CONTENTS

Foreword – Tom Gardner	3
Acknowledgements	6
Introduction	8
1 The Decision to Leave	11
2 Understanding Yourself	18
3 Prepare Your Finances	33
4 The Job Market: Hunt, Compete, Achieve	43
5 Negotiate, negotiate, negotiate	71
6 Education	84
7 Networking	98
8 Basic Business Structures	113
9 Novel ideas for job seekers	134
10 The Economy and Industries	141
11 Workplace Integration	163
12 Specific skills and areas to consider	174
Your Future	184
References	186
	191
About The Author	191

FOREWORD – TOM GARDNER

In 1995 a new adventure began. After 20 years in the military (3 years infantry, 2 years medical corps, 15 years in the special forces and 2 wars) and not knowing anything other than the US Army way of life, I decided to retire and spend time with my family. This decision took it's toll in ways I had not expected from day one. I had done so much, helped so many, and travelled to so many different countries. I had met Presidents, Ambassadors, Princes and so many great people. At the time I felt important, but that all changed when the military was cut away. When the day came to leave the Army, I had no plan. I took the first job that was offered to me, in construction, as a labourer. On my first day as a civilian I was in an old swimming pool with a jack hammer breaking up concrete and removing the pieces. All I could think of was that this was how my future would look! I had gone from being a well-trained special forces operator to breaking up concrete. For the next couple of weeks all I could think about was that I had made a terrible mistake. It was as if I had just taken a 20-year vacation and I was trying to start my life all over again. Nothing I had done during that time appeared to have any relevance to my civilian life.

I once read a quote that said: *"The military teaches you how to be a Soldier, but they don't teach you how to be a civilian"* and for me that was so true. I decided to apply what I had learned and set goals. The first was to get out of the pool. I found a contract role using my military (radio) communication skills with a computer company supporting the US Army. After that I obtained a teaching position which saw me teaching the next generation of young officer candidates. Following that I managed to gain a position with a telecommunications company in New York City. Two years into the job in New York, 9/11 happened. I contemplated going back to the Service but reflected on how far I had come in my new life and decided to keep moving forward even though the temptation to deviate from my plan was great.

I moved to a position working for a contractor supporting the US Army weapons development program. After a year in this environment I realised that I had the skills and confidence to start my own business. In 2005, some 10 years after leaving the US Army, I decided to take the risk and establish my own company. Not having any real business background, I found this a lot harder than I make it sound now! There were a lot of highs and lows over the next 15 years. At one point things went so badly that I had to move my office into my basement and work using a plywood table as my desk. I found ways to apply the skills I had learned in the military in this new environment. In this case the basic message was to never to give up. I just kept setting goals and moving towards them. By starting my company, I found many of the same traits and skills I learned in the Army carried through to building and maintaining a business. Loyalty, pride and a sense of accomplishment were just some of the emotions that I re-connected with. Starting a company and keeping it going has been one of the most difficult but rewarding achievements in my life. The military taught me how to persevere, an enduring trait which can traverse so many aspects of life and one which I will always appreciate.

Remember: "There is Life after Service" - find what you like and do it!

Tom Gardner
SFC (RET) United States Army Special Forces
CEO and Entrepeneur

ACKNOWLEDGEMENTS

This book is very much a personal perspective on transition, but it has been made possible by having the stable and unwavering support of my family and friends. Without a stable transition out of the military I could not have written it.

Tom Gardner, who contributed the foreword, has been a great support as I made the decisions leading to departure from the military. Graeme Campbell, my business partner, has been instrumental in so many ways that I shan't embarrass him by listing them here. His family have been equally supportive when they had no reason to be, other than their own profound sense of kindness.

There are contributors who are not recorded in print but who have shaped my views, helped me target my research and inspired me to make this book as useful as I hope it can be. Dean, a former infantier who I will not fully identify, knows who he is. I will never forget his words; "why aren't there any books showing how you can transition with dignity, that soldiers can put down a rifle and start negotiating deals". Huw Lloyd, whose friendship and support as I moved my life to a new place and an entirely new career has been instrumental. My good friends and former colleagues Hamish Findlay and Paul Melling, both aviation experts in their own right and now forging successful second careers of their own.

My sister Chelsey, whose contribution on adult education later in the book shows how many opportunities are there to be

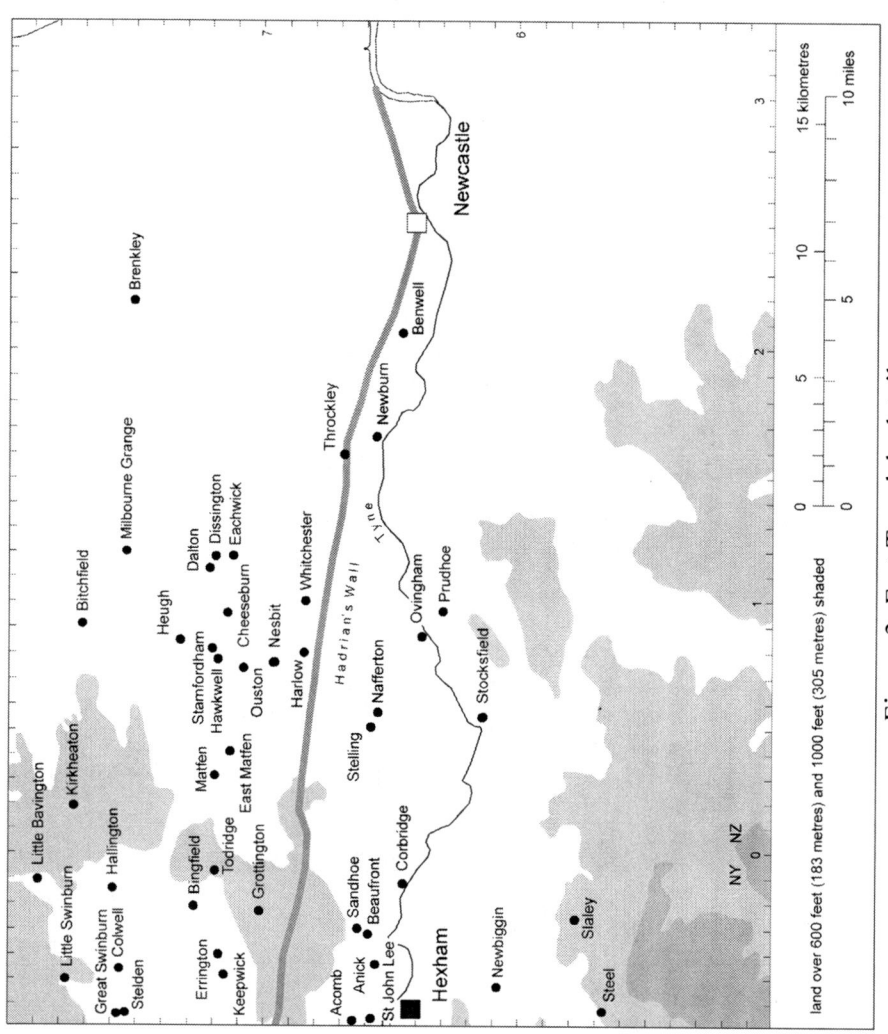

Figure 3: East Tynedale detail

grasped. Her own academic credentials are far superior to any of mine. Last but not least, my mother Candy. For surviving my military career with me over the phone, from Afghanistan to the Arctic.

INTRODUCTION

If you are reading this book it is likely that you are on the cusp of leaving the military after what has probably been a life-changing period.

Perhaps you feel cynical. Perhaps you feel excited. You probably feel scared -you have what my colleagues and I used to call "the fear" – that healthy urge to explore what you don't think you understand while still being aware that your military career has come with significant benefits.

I started writing this book one month before I officially resigned from the Naval Service. I had made the decision a two years in advance but went through a range of emotions, life experiences and financial changes which kept me in a little bit longer. "I'll just do one more job." "It's only 2 more years." These phrases are valid and sometimes the right ones to consider. Other times they are not.

There is never a perfect time to make a change like this one. The text I will share with you is purely my own view, a combination of experience from advising those I was lucky enough to have charge of and my own often uncompromising experiences. I apply some academic rigour to my assertions, but not to the point where you are swamped with references from literary works. What might help you, though, is taking just one snippet of what I write in this book. Advice costs very little but making your own decisions in a well-informed manner adds value.

Treat this short book as a pocket-sized guide. If you aren't sure of something, skip to the chapter that sounds like it will help the most. If it doesn't answer your question comprehensively it will give you a good steer. You do not need to read this book from cover to cover to build your plan to transition into civilian life but it does run in the order that I planned mine.

The chapters are structured to match the feelings I experienced as I went through various stages. In broad terms these were:

- the decision to leave
- the realisation that I needed to educate myself
- emotional development and aims
- testing the job market
- re-assessment of my aims
- job applications
- starting a business

Some themes run through all of these stages, such as the need to build a network, the need to continue to deliver in my existing role and a desire to improve my commercial awareness. Throughout each stage I will explain how I managed these issues while also drawing on some examples from colleagues in different situations. In that sense I hope this work can apply to you, even if our circumstances are different.

For me, the hardest part was not leaving but in fact understanding the type of person I am. I joined the Royal Navy shortly after my 19th birthday. I was flying helicopters by 21 and fully qualified by 22. These were aims I had held since my early teens. After 8 years, I was 70% inclined to stay in the Service, whilst 30% of me wanted to leave. Some 3 years later, those numbers had swapped places. Understanding the reasons for the change is the foundation of the plan that resulted and the reason I can still feel fulfilled.

This guide will not comment on the benefits of a military career, or any perception that these have increased or reduced. This book is helpful if you are considering leaving or have already made the decision but want to better understand the path ahead. Similarly, you may have been a civilian for some time but want a different perspective on specific topics. This book aims to be a hand-rail maximising your chances of future success.

I thoroughly enjoyed my military career. It developed qualities in my character which I find very useful in business. The enduring characteristic which we all share and which we can nurture is to persevere. Never give up, no matter how difficult things get or how challenging your goals appear. You might take some sidesteps, you might go backwards occasionally, but whatever happens find a way to move forward and do not stop. I left on a personal high and I attribute that to having a plan and making sure I kept forward momentum. Through reading this book I hope I can help you do the same, or better.

1 THE DECISION TO LEAVE

You have decided that your time in the military is coming to an end. The reasons might seem clear but I would suggest that they run deeper than you will admit.

Let us first consider your situation. In my experience, those leaving fall into one of only a few general categories:

- **Those who have reached a pensionable age.**
- **Those who seek more independence (a perception of freedom).**
- **Those who felt they had "seen the best" of the possible military roles on offer.**
- **Those under personal pressure.**

If you feel disillusioned it is probably linked to one of the above points. It is not enough to simply say "I've had enough, I'm off." Have you had enough because you can't deal with a strict regime anymore? Bullet point two applies. Have you had enough because your partner is threatening to leave you and you are also bored of your job? Points three and four apply. Once you have decided to leave establish truthfully why you have reached this conclusion. This will come in useful later when you plan your next move.

If you can't specify the reason for your negative feeling, you may be going through a low patch. Be wary of this when making rash decisions about your career. Giving a decision like this time might offer more clarity than simply handing in your resignation on a whim.

If you analyse yourself, you are likely to find the previous four points apply to you to varied degrees. You might have a strong desire for independence and have little interest in the pension offer you will be sacrificing. If you want independence it is likely that you desire more risk which possibly means you don't have financially dependent children. These assumptions generally follow each other logically and acknowledging them (rather than hiding from them) will help you.

Once the decision is made but before you offer your voluntary redundancy I recommend talking to both your immediate superior, your career manager, and your local base welfare representative. This serves a number of purposes. It is true that some or all of these individuals will try and convince you to stay. I recommend that you respect this approach regardless of your views. Those you are speaking to have a professional duty to keep the Armed Forces well-staffed and ready. A degree of respect for that role will help to keep doors open as you move into a new life. You might find yourself serving as a reservist alongside the same people; you might set up a business and recruit them; you might end up working for the same firm. You might also want to explore the option of re-joining and being disruptive during your departure will not help this possible course of action.

The outcomes I describe might seem very unlikely but you may be surprised at how situations can develop. I have found success in taking a long-term view of any situation. A kind word now along with some respect and a steadfast approach to work until your last day of service will reap dividends in ways that are not obvious now.

Leaving interviews offer another chance to re-assess your decision and ensure that your future courses of action are mapped out. Occasionally you may receive advice on subjects you were not expecting such as economic stability, the job market and family life. Remember that these individuals are discharging their duty and trying to help. I remember a time when I advised a sailor after he wasn't on the promotion list and he decided that day to submit his voluntary redundancy request. He was understandably annoyed and disillusioned. After some discussion he remained in the Naval Service and I found out he was leaving four years later. I am as confident now as I was then that in four years he learnt more, saved more money and did more to develop himself. I am glad that he continued serving after our meeting but I am equally pleased he decided to leave on his own terms.

As with my advice to that sailor, take all information as it is intended and question where appropriate. When I initially resigned (in a slightly rash move; I withdrew my resignation and did re-submitted it two years later) I was counselled on Brexit, the value of the pound, inflation and private sector employment. I did not take this advice well. At the time I was looking at finance sector roles and had done considerable evening study. I found the subsequent advice patronising. Reflecting now I was wrong to take such a position. What if Brexit did damage the financial sector? How would that affect my job seeking? Were there alternatives? Do not disregard any advice but do apply intelligence before you act on it.

You will be offered numerous options. These will depend on your length of service and seniority in rank. I will not go through every possible outcome in this book. The re-settlement office at your unit is resourced to offer in-depth advice on your options. You need to take time to understand what these are and ask as many questions as necessary before deciding on which course of action to take. Hopefully it will be the most beneficial for your personal and future career circumstances. This guide will help you navigate the course you choose.

Many factors will influence your decision-making process during this early stage. My first act was to compare my level of formal education with those who were applying for roles I had an interest in. My advice is to always assume you need more education, whether formal or informal. Learning is your insurance policy. It is what will keep you competitive in the job market, keep you sane and it will help you develop as a thinker. Making full use of the resources on offer while you are still serving will help you to boost any perceived gaps in your educational credentials. I will discuss this in more detail in a later chapter.

What I have termed "The Geography of Leaving" is worthy of note. The way you employ resources (time, savings, re-settlement opportunities) will be affected by numerous factors. These can be linked back to the four core reasons for leaving but they are also influenced by physical location. For example, a junior rating or non-commissioned officer who has their last posting in Plymouth Dockyard, or perhaps Catterick Garrison, will have a very different set of opportunities to a Lieutenant Colonel whose last military role is in London. The reasons for this are straightforward. London has networking clubs (both military and non-military), a higher average earnings level and an abundance of young companies looking for ambitious and articulate employees. Helpfully other cities and sectors of industry are setting up their own networking events and clubs, so the situation is constantly improving. There are also techniques you can use to level the playing field even if you find yourself leaving from an isolated base location.

There are many opportunities outside London and regional cities are constantly improving their networking opportunities. If the nuclear industry appeals you could exceed the earnings of a junior investment banker without moving to a major city. In terms of sector specifics the same applies to procurement (Bristol), aerospace and engineering (Derbyshire, Cheshire, Deeside, Avon), Defence (nationwide). Your options are plentiful but they need to refinement to make the most of your situation. Your flexibility will be tested regardless. Managers in companies large and small are often expected to travel to win business, check on clients or oversee the commercial operations of their firm. Those willing to move at short notice are likely to be highly sought after. The opposite can also be true, particularly for deep technical specialists whose place of work may be far more easily predictable based purely on their skill set. In my case the more general the role, the more travel was required. Exceptions to this exist but it is a good metric against which to plan your own time and education.

Later we will examine the sectors a service leaver might consider. Further research will highlight where these particular sectors are concentrated. This is useful if you have served predominantly in a particular region. Your family and personal roots will also have a major influence. Whatever situation the general rules and themes highlighted in this book can be used to give you maximum advantage.

At the time of writing the standard notice period for a service leaver is twelve months, to include leave periods and resettlement activity. A year to find another role sounds like a long time. By commercial standards, it is. In many sectors it is possible to lose your job very quickly and businesses are often keen to lose those personnel who have expressed a desire to move on. Whereas the military is constantly recruiting efficient businesses are run with the minimal number of staff required to maximise profit while ensuring safety. Those leaving could take with them commercial secrets, disenfranchise remaining staff and generally create disruption. If you are still serving you retain the comfort of knowing that your salary is guaranteed for twelve months. When devoting every part of your spare capacity to setting yourself up for success this final year will pass quickly. Before long your time for dedicated learning is over and your CV is being circulated.

While serving there are opportunities to make the most of this stability in your final months. Dedicating a little more time to study, reflection and planning will pay dividends. There will be a temptation to maintain the same social norms and levels of personal spending in your final year, driven by a perception that you should not have to drastically change the things you enjoy. I recommend considering a gradual change during this period, starting in the first few months after you resign. Look for small ways to change your routines that incorporate learning and saving. This will best prepare you for unforeseen changes. By the time you leave you need to be geared for full time work or highly effective job seeking if you are to minimise the time spent without employment or income.

The journey you are embarking on is a blend of your deepest inner thoughts, your mental and physical abilities and your risk appetite. Understanding how your mind and body work and how these elements interact is challenging, but the closer you are to refining each part the greater your potential impact. The easy route will appeal in the more difficult moments but this is seldom the route to take. If you do not want to do yourself justice and maximise your life opportunities, then this book is not for you.

2 UNDERSTANDING YOURSELF

Why did you join the military? Think about what that decision meant to you. Was it patriotism? Adventure? Friendship? Stability? Or to prepare yourself for something else?

Like your reasons for leaving, your reasons for joining are likely to be a combination of these things. Never under-estimate or under-sell what you were part of. You sacrificed parts of your own basic liberty to support a wider cause. This choice and lifestyle take a certain level of robustness, fortitude and mental capacity. It is fair to say that you possess some or all of these qualities.

I noticed during my own transition a desire by military people to describe "leadership and management" as their key skill. This always confused me a little when considered alongside my studies of business and financial principles. If we assume the main purpose of business is to generate revenue and to generate revenue businesses need to co-ordinate resources to produce outputs, an ability to lead and manage clearly contributes. The problem I have with the suggestion that leadership and management are qualifications to guarantee outputs is that it is not specific enough.

Imagine the following in the context of an interview for a management role with a large food processing business:

Interviewer: "We have two shifts of ten people running twelve hours in twenty-four on a processed flour production line. Our marginal costs are starting to cripple us, and our fixed costs have increased seven percent year on year for the last five years. We need to stop the marginal cost increases, but still honour our existing contracts which we think were badly priced. The bank is also calling in our short-term liabilities earlier than planned. What should we do?"

Applicant: "We should examine leadership in the production line teams and see if it can be strengthened. We should also look at the management styles of the team leaders."

Interviewer: "Ok. How will that tangibly stop marginal cost increases and keep the bank at bay regarding our short-term debt?"

What do you think? I admit it, this is a coarse example and if you are sitting through a job interview like this one I hope the rewards if you succeed reflect the complexity of the challenge! In order to succeed in the long term you cannot rely on the provenance of your military experience entirely. That experience will get you noticed and may instil confidence, but if you want to succeed and achieve your goals you need wider choice. To achieve wider choice you need to understand who you are.

I will now outline the process I went through in understanding myself, shaped by my network of advisers, my friends and family and by my financial limitations. Your experience will be different but the following text will offer some useful pointers.

Firstly, imagine your future situation. Pick something close enough to visualise, but not so far ahead that it is unimaginable (maybe four years). Note that down. Secondly, imagine that tomorrow, you win five million pounds through a lottery entry. What would you do with the money in the context of your medium-term ambition?

When I did this, the following options came to mind:

Question One (future medium-term goal): Running my own business.

Question Two (winning five million pounds): Investing to grow the business I want to run.

This will then lead to other questions. For me, they were:

What sort of business do I want to run?

How long do I want to run it for?

Based on these two points, how would I invest capital resource (money) to achieve these goals?

What is the minimum I need to maintain an acceptable standard of living? (Assuming that after I achieve this standard I invest whatever is left of my five million pounds in the business).

This first step was the beginning of my journey to changing my course and to doing what I wanted. My conclusions focus on self-employment. From this we can conclude from chapter one that my main reason for leaving the Armed Forces was a desire for personal independence.

Let us consider what would be different if my answers had been the following:

Question One (future medium-term goal): A professional earning the equivalent salary to that which I would have made in-service (including pension contributions).

Question Two (winning five million pounds): Retire and spend time with my family.

These answers show a different but equally valid approach. In this second case stability is important. This individual has things they aren't willing to risk losing. This could be a dependent family, a property, their reputation or social status. They desire a stable plan into retirement as early as possible. They are willing to give up resources (their time and energy) to make profit for someone else in exchange for a stable and predictable reward. In this sense, they are looking for similar benefits to a military career, without the separation from home.

There is another option distinct from the others:

Question One (future medium-term goal): I want to have a positive impact on my family/society/the world.

Question Two (winning five million pounds): Use this resource to improve/accelerate the way I make a positive change.

This motivation is more subtle. Here, the positive impact is undefined. Notice how in the previous two examples the aims of the individual are specific. Running a business and from that finding a desired financial level or offering stability and predictability to a situation versus broader positive change. In fact in this latest example, both of the aims could sit within the answer to Question one. In order to have a positive impact you need to sustain yourself and offer your part of the family support (which could be shared or done by you entirely). Without this foundation you may find it very difficult to create the spare capacity you need to have a positive impact on anything. The same can be said of Question two. In this scenario the cash boost of a lottery win does not change your desire to create change.

This exercise is a simple way to identify your personal ideology and then immediately test it by offering almost unlimited alternative choices. In my case personal ideology is very important. It is the reason I make decisions the way I do and I guard my ideology closely. That is not to suggest that my perspective is always the right one, but identifying a personal ideology and then testing it by seeking out alternatives is a useful exercise. If your mind is changed then perhaps your original ideology wasn't so strong after all?

If in the previous exercise you found yourself conflicted or unsure, fear not. You do not have to transition to the civilian world of work with a cast iron belief in yourself and an unshakeable sense of your path. Trying to understand the route to such self-belief simply offers a way to better understand the intricacies of your character with a military environment removed.

Let us consider the military system that many of us have served in. Helpfully it shares attributes with other large organisations. As such the lessons may offer useful perspective even if you have been in the civilian workplace for some time. The military is a machine. It's inputs (in the United Kingdom) are public sector finance, a labour force and strategy. From these three inputs cascade equipment, planning, institutional structures and all other manner of functions down to a sailor on a frigate or a soldier in the field. The feed-back loops (processes allowing evaluation of a task or system, good or bad, and change to be implemented) are generally short between the shallower hierarchical layers meaning that the influence of those immediately above or below your own rank can happen quickly. In the case of ranks more removed in seniority terms such feedback happens at a slower pace. The level of investment by the organisation in the individual is generally higher than most other equivalently large organisations.

How does this system influence your thinking? In my case it strengthened a resolve to take risks knowing that I had the backing of a larger body; it cemented friendships which made me value loyalty above almost all other feelings; it made financial gain a secondary or even tertiary consideration. These factors change as our norms are refined with age and our circumstances evolve, but the foundational elements remain.

Now let us consider a hypothetical multi-national corporation. Like the military it has financing (investors) and labour. Like the military, it is a machine. Finances are managed to co-ordinate resources which are in turn employed to create products and/or services that generate further financial gain. In its most basic form, for the business to survive, the equation is simple:

Revenue (money earned) must exceed Cost (money spent) to result in Profit

Through this overview we see that the military and a large company have similar core attributes. Now overlay your own personal ideology onto both organisations. Your understanding of where your ideology sits in a military context is likely to be strong, but in a privately run organisation (unless you have prior knowledge) it is likely to be weaker. The same may be said of an insurance broker looking to transfer into agricultural management, or a blacksmith trying to change skills and work as an NHS manager. Your innermost driving forces will both consciously and sub-consciously affect the decisions you make to solve this problem.

When I drew conclusions for my future it felt like a swift process. In fact it took me approximately one year. I wanted to be an investment banker (because I wanted to maximise my earning potential). I did not consider the deeper question of why I wanted more money. I simply decided that after a reasonably intense military career that a demanding role in a new area was what I should aspire to. Financial services roles (particularly client facing) are very different to those you may have been exposed to in the public sector. They are hard won, hard earning jobs where substantial remuneration and extravagance often mask difficult decision making and many hours of work. My lesson was that if my aim was to make money there had to be a deeper reason, personal or otherwise, for doing so.

Doing something because you feel it is expected of you even if you do not truly want to can lead to some interesting places. At worst, you will end up doing something you dislike intensely and at best, you will plough through this stage and adjust. There is nothing wrong with these approaches, but I suspect you can do better with good preparation and an intrinsic knowledge of your inner desires and capabilities.

I hope that you are now closer to understanding what you really want and have some extra tools to further develop your ideas. This process is often a slow and painful one and I encourage you to speak to family and friends as you progress. In addition (and if you can) reach out to those working in different industries to better understand their roles and lifestyles. There is an art to doing this if you want to make connections. There is also a skill in receiving the resulting information, monitoring who you have responded to and the tracking stage of each relationship. I will outline techniques on all of the above in the networking chapter

Once your aims are refined the next step will be to understand how achievable they are based on your current position. Think of yourself as a formed body of men and women in a military unit. Each part is trained to a basic level, and then specialised in certain areas to provide functions that the formed mass cannot; logistics, engineering, operations and medical. Now apply this model to yourself in light of your own ambitions. You have your brain, fitness, emotional senses and appearance. Within each of these you have education, physical strengths, diet, sleep patterns, the skills you enjoy, the skills you do not. Conduct self-analysis to understand your capabilities. Mine were as follows:

Mind, energy, appearance, personal network

These can be broken down into specific sub-categories as follows:

Mind: Numeracy, literacy, adaptability, communications, problem solving. This is your operations room, your academic centre of mass and an organ that you can keep improving indefinitely. Do not underestimate how powerful your mind is compared to everything else. You might have significant formal qualification or indeed have very few at all. Regardless, your ability to grow your mental capacity is important in both cases. Keep your mind active and seek out challenges for it to reap the rewards later on.

Energy: Diet, Sleep, Motivation. These can often be over-looked by those of us with a mindset is objective focussed. Sleep is to be respected and if properly supported by diet it forms a core part of your capabilities. It will also restore and maintain your capacity if things become challenging.

Appearance: Haircut, Smartness of Clothing, Posture, Presence. This suggestion should not imply that great expense is required. Simple things can build towards creating a presence when you are in the company of new people. Some suggest that bright clothing or looking drastically different will help you stand out. It will, but it may not be the optimum approach. Instead I recommend the basics that you likely already know. I recommend clean shoes, ironed clothes and sharp, single tone colours. Posture is important because it will make you feel more confident if you stand correctly. This will add to your presence, an intangible and sometimes awkward subject. Your aim should be for others to remember you but in an understated and respectful manner. Interviews and interactions still rely on body language and first impressions which are often based on appearance and bearing. Automated job selection may eventually remove humans from recruitment and vetting, but until then be prepared to put your best foot forward in every sense.

Personal Network: Breadth, Time, Gaps, Growth Potential, Utility. Your military connections offer you a ready made network. While powerful many of those you know may still be serving which will offer limited help in your career search. Networking groups for all ranks are now commonplace and if complemented by your own activity can offer great utility. Using the self-analysis techniques discussed earlier consider those sectors which appeal the most and those that you do not wish to consider. I will discuss network planning later in some detail but at this stage consider that you need a system for growing your network, maintaining it and politely disengaging from those parts that offer no assistance. Every connection made could lead to at least two more with dedicated effort. As such, effort with five contacts could grow to ten. Then twenty. Then forty? This rate of growth is not sustainable and a balance of effort over output must be struck. Proper management can lead to positive results. This is your personal communications strategy and it should be treated as a foundational part of your transition.

Things you cannot do without

A useful secondary exercise is to then identify the parts of your life where you cannot compromise or have a low risk tolerance. While obvious, having them front and centre is a useful handbrake to elaborate or un-realistic planning.

Family, home, reputation

Reputation is an intangible part of your being, unlike your home and family. Despite this it's value cannot be underestimated. In any self-analysis reputation should be kept at the forefront of future decision making. Any perception that reputation can be side lined or ignored is, in my experience, mistaken. Your reputation will be the glue that binds future success together. Yours may seem insignificant, but if you achieve your aims, you will inevitably build one that is more powerful. You may be familiar with the phrase "you make your own luck." I have always interpreted this as "your reputation attracts opportunity." Compromise here may lead to stagnation or at worst failure in the long-term. The importance of home and family are self-explanatory but are different in each individual case.

The protection of reputation, home and family will be instrumental in your approach to career and lifestyle changes. I labour the importance of reputation in particular because there are many examples of individuals who have fallen from grace by ignoring the importance of this key element. This is disappointing and can lead to lost opportunity. As such, protect your reputation and try to engage only in things which will strengthen it. Surrounding yourself with others who share a similar level of integrity and honesty will assist you.

Understanding your inner driving forces can offer great value and pausing to consider them can offer great strength. It can be visceral, enjoyable, painful and liberating. Learning about yourself is akin to the fitness test you dread or the heavy pack you can't carry further, the deployment you want to come home from or the family events you wish you'd been around for. It is an inevitable part of the life you are choosing, just as those feelings were a part of the one you are potentially leaving. You persevered beyond the challenges of your military career and this new experience requires the same fortitude.

The pace of your self-analysis can be controlled. You can slow down if you start to question your value systems or perhaps changing your ways of thinking in unexpected ways. Equally this process can reinforce long held beliefs, often comforting when change is everywhere. If you are interested in conducting deeper personal analysis I recommend "What Colour is your Parachute" by Richard Bolles[1]. This work goes into great detail and has been used by numerous colleagues to refine their future path. An Army colleague of mine used it in his final years of service to great effect.

The stages so far discussed run as follows:

What is your four-year plan? Would infinite choice change this plan?

What are your core attributes that you wish to support, optimise and develop?

What are you unwilling to sacrifice and therefore protect?

If you can answer these questions you have a foundation from which your success can be built. You should have a sense of your risk appetite, the core attributes that result, and the things that cannot be lost. Now you need to make sure your finances and those of others can support your plan.

Harsh realities

In my experience most people in the United Kingdom who exercise rational thought respect military service and the notion that those who have served have sacrificed something. In some rare cases one can experience antagonism and misplaced pity. It is very important to consider your actions and behaviour carefully when encountering a negative perception.

Many people cling to what has gone before and some former military personnel are no different. This is particularly true for those who moved into civilian life and not achieved goals which matched the status or excitement they perceived when serving.

If you find yourself slipping into this mindset, consider those who did not join the military but live very challenging lives, often with far less recognition. The National Health Service has hundreds of thousands of such people, as do the emergency services, private companies and those living as full-time carers. It would be easy to make unsophisticated arguments about military career achievements in comparison to those who have not served. Doing so will achieve little and also create division where none is necessary. Your move into the professional world that the majority occupy cannot be characterised by your perceptions of your military status. Better to become an example to those still serving and an inspiration for those leaving than a cynic.

Your military training gives you competitive advantage in many areas but this must be viewed in context. It also exposes you to flaws and weaknesses that must be managed carefully. I was recently talking to a friend about writing this book. He was an infantry reconnaissance platoon sniper whose tour of Afghanistan makes mine look pedestrian. We discussed how on occasion others assume we experienced things so harrowing that we must need therapy.

This type of discussion comes from one of a number of perspectives, some well-meaning and others ignorant. The adage "every man thinks meanly of himself for not having been a soldier, or not having been at sea"[2] can play a small part. Equally you might interact with individuals who have a limited knowledge of current affairs or the deeper purposes behind international conflict and peacekeeping. Hopefully you are talking to someone who has a genuine concern for your wellbeing. My friend and I agreed that the best way to deal with such an approach is a reasoned discussion (or indeed acceptance of help if required).

This is true of any interaction with someone whom you aren't close to, whether a job interviewer, a new partner or a new colleague. A sub-optimal outcome would be to react aggressively out of a sense of protection for the principles and friends that you hold dear. In order to change perceptions and change any dubious third-party opinion, try to be methodical. Do not overreact, swear or try to make those you are speaking to feel guilty. Be honest, explain whether you do indeed suffer from the long-term effects of conflict and hold your head up. You don't deserve to be spoken to like a broken animal, but equally, those who know no better deserve a fair chance to receive a different perspective. Re-aligning negative perception is a long-term effort by all those who have served and continue to serve.

Perceptions of status

It is unfortunate to hear of colleagues who have left at the pinnacle of highly specialised careers only to find themselves disillusioned or in a struggle to find the right role. The problem is often with the perceptions of those who take the roles on.

Some of my most successful friends took on roles that many would ignore or think beneath them. Despite this, the lessons learned shaped a future that has seen them overtake the more "conventional" model. You can move out of the military in a number of ways but I recommend a long-term goal that allows for short-term friction.

In terms of third part perception, my aim is to be known as an Entrepreneur whose military background is not obvious. In my case this goal is the hallmark of un-restricted success; to move from an institution and become an institution in yourself. For those reading this who know me, I still have some way to go!

The ex-military community needs inspirational people known for their non-military work to showcase the positive impact of change and the happiness that comes with a varied career. It is on all of us to make the most of our capability in civilian life for the benefit of each other.

3 PREPARE YOUR FINANCES

A strong financial position leads to choice and allows flexible, agile decision making. This enables you to identify opportunities as they arise and seize them. That doesn't imply extreme wealth from the outset. Your specific funds are only one part of your plan to make the most of them.

Your finances are likely to be the driving force behind almost every decision you make. This statement may at first seem simplistic, particularly if you hold yourself to the mantra that money doesn't bring you happiness. The arguments for the role money plays in our behaviours and lifestyle choices are complex and are determined by external factors (national culture, financial rates of interest, inflation) as well as internal ones (our personal spending norms, ability to save, willingness to take financial risk). The influences are complex and each one is intertwined with the others in ways that you may be unfamiliar with.

This means that financial decisions we make every day have longer-term positive and negative effects that may not seem obvious.

The decision to buy a new car on finance may prevent you taking a different, unexpected opportunity in two years. Equally, buying an unreliable car for a low cash sum may result in you missing a job interview due to a roadside breakdown! As such, consider the possible courses of action that each financial decision could open or close. Taking a decision (the new car in this case) may commit you to thousands of pounds in interest payments over the term of your ownership. The investments you could have made with that money and the growth you could have experienced (but now cannot), is known in economic terms as the "opportunity cost". Considering opportunity cost is a useful way of deciding which decision is right for you.

Stability and decision making

Holding a financial reserve will calm your thinking and allow reasoned decision making. The level of reserve depends on your aspirations, costs of living and non-discretionary commitments. This final point is worthy of some analysis.

The military is famous (sometimes infamous!) for its social bonds and for groups of like-minded people who share social situations that are uncommon in other professions. This often leads to behaviours which make the most of the disposable income a military career is able to offer. Problems that could be solved with a refined approach are solved using exiting funds with little scrutiny of other options. These are discretionary behaviours and they can cost significant sums (relative to most incomes). Cutting down on eating out, alcohol and weekends away will not appeal to some but it will build financial resilience and give more time to prepare your future.

Non-discretionary spending and behaviour is that which you simply cannot change or stop without risking significant damage to your situation. This includes mortgage repayments, food, utilities and any childcare or other dependant family spending. When budgeting for the future these commitments should form the core of your financial requirements. Short-term debt may also be included whether on un-secured loans, credit cards or assets like cars and furniture. I am not a financial adviser and so will not give advice on how to manage these assets as part of your wider cost of living. Instead I recommend that you consider your situation to identify that spending which is essential and minimise all else until your transition plan bears fruit.

Your financial position

Once you have considered the previous factors your monthly, weekly and even daily cost of living can be calculated. It is the norm to aspire to a higher quality of life than your present one, so take these figures and decide how much more money you require (perhaps for savings, holidays or other opportunities). This will indicate the approximate gross salary you wish to command on leaving the military as well as a minimum earning level which you can use in a salary negotiation.

For example, you could calculate the cost of your mortgage, food, utilities and personal transport each month. In this instance let us say the total is £1700. In a month with twenty available weekdays in which to work this amounts to £85 a day of earning required. Now let us add an "emergency savings" fund of £400 per month and a private pension plan of £125 per month. This gives a total monthly requirement of £2225, or in our 20 day month, £111.25 per day of earnings required. The equivalent salary is £26,700 before tax.

If your financial position is healthy, you may wish to consider how your options change if you accept a reduction in income for a defined amount of time. Consider the following; a service leaver, who feels comfortable as a project manager, takes a role in a regional utilities company. They earn a salary of £40,000, with a contributory workplace pension and a company car (in real terms worth £350 a month). The organisation offers steady progression, and after five years a project manager can expect to command a salary of £55,000.

In a different scenario, a service leaver decides to change tack completely and become a financial analyst. They earn less than £30,000 a year and are expected to live in a major city, such as London or Birmingham, where the cost of living is significantly higher than for our project manager. This individual may have to supplement their monthly income from savings, will be more junior in the organisation and has a lower quality of life than if they became a project manager.

In five years, however, the financial analyst has learned their new industry and become credible. They have promoted, and this promotion leads to a salary of £75,000 with a performance-based bonus. Who is better off?

In fact neither is "better off" in a holistic sense, they have simply taken different paths to a stable position. Both view success differently and both are able to turn that vision into reality. The difference is, without a stable savings base to fall back on, our financial analyst may have had far fewer choices at the outset. This shows how our financial decision making may close future doors, depending on our willingness to accept risk or personal austerity. Once you have calculated your "bare minimum" earnings, consider your savings and calculate how often they could be used to supplement your earnings and for how long. This may open more options for your future employment, but with the caveats that there will be a time limit on how long you can endure that position for.

A military pension may factor for many reading this book. A pension is a powerful tool which provides both financial stability and a psychological safety net. A pension can equally lull you into a false sense of security. Remember, in crude terms, that a pension of approximately £12,000 per year is the equivalent of a number of other investments that could be made if your savings support them. That doesn't mean you should disregard the benefits of a guaranteed workplace pension. It is simply an illustration of how the stability of a pension can be replicated in other ways provided you plan far enough ahead. When I resigned I was approximately nine years away from an officers' pension at twenty one years of service. I felt that there were greater opportunities to use my skills both for personal development and financial gain away from the Service. That may not prove to be true, but my plan is more concerned with building a successful business than comparing my potential position in future years.

If you are in a difficult financial situation, consider carefully your decision to leave the military. Might it be worth waiting until things stabilise? Perhaps another year of service will allow you to clear your short-term debt or finish a qualification. John Maynard Keynes, a world-famous British economist, described stock market shocks such as the great depression as being fuelled by "Animal Spirits".[3] That is to say that human behaviour, rather than pure mathematical logic, can create a condition where a situation is much worse as people panic and start to suspect an impending catastrophe. He was describing how ordinary people withdrew their savings fearing that their money would be lost by their banks. This in turn gave retail banks less money to lend against to their commercial clients and brought economic collapse more quickly and extremely. Consider your own "Animal Spirits" during your transition to the civilian workplace. What fuels them, and how does this modify your financial decision making? If you can understand your behaviour in those circumstance you are in a stronger position than someone who cannot.

Financial basics to grasp

In the Armed Forces, your tax is paid before you know it (known as Pay As You Earn, PAYE) as is your national insurance and your pension which, though non-contributory at the time of writing, has a monthly figure attached to it by the government. When you leave, you may have to fill out a self-assessment tax return (some of you will already do this) and understand what you can offset as tax-deductible allowances.

There are also tax efficient savings schemes that are worthy of consideration, both for yourself and your family. An ISA allows you to save money at a higher interest rate than a standard bank account, and you do not pay tax the resulting interest payments. Early on in your career, this may not seem relevant but over ten or twenty years these small amounts build to what can become a useful savings buffer. This feeds back into your stable financial position allowing flexible and agile decision making.

There are financial term which I would recommend a basic understanding of. These include:

-Inflation and Deflation

-Interest Rates (including both the effects of simple and compound interest)

-Exchange Rates (particularly your own currency against two other major trading partners, such as the US Dollar or Euro)

-Gross Domestic Product (GDP)

-Investment Yield (the amount of money you receive from an investment expressed as a percentage of the original amount).

These terms may be new to some readers and only a basic understanding is required to get started. These terms affect everything you interact with, from your mortgage, your car, your holidays and salary. You cannot escape their impact if you live in a capitalist economy and in trade terms they influence non-capitalist ones too. Knowing the basic principles of each will help you make a myriad of decisions, from what type of mortgage to apply for to when is best to buy a car. More importantly, these factors all influence businesses. Showing a basic awareness of what they mean in an interview or informal discussion will set you apart as someone who is invested in their future and can be trusted to learn new skills when required. If you aspire to a financial services career, these items are the bare minimum I would consider understanding before going further.

Finance can be complex and professional advice is often a worthwhile investment. An accountant can explain how your finances, particularly your tax, are affected by your decision making and investments. This may seem daunting at first but is often the safest way forward when planning major financial changes. The same can be said of a good solicitor. It is difficult to be an expert in all fields and time spent learning skills you could rely on an expert for is time lost for your main goals (unless the two happen to be the same). A general understanding of the terms and topics covered here will help to protect you from poor advice rather than give you detailed answers.

What is your risk threshold?

Risk is by nature highly subjective. Our threshold to expose the things we care about to risk will vary based on experience, emotional capacity and financial stability. I have included this section in the finances chapter as I believe the two are closely intertwined, but risk touches on every part of your decision-making processes.

Taking risk is often glamorised by the media, whether in terms of physicality, gambling or those willing to break the law to achieve a life-changing fate. With a regular bombardment of glamorous risk taking it is easy to see how some people may be lured into decision making patterns which, in turn, lead to disaster. Reacting to this situation is a balance between finding inspiration from the risks taken around you while also recognising the folly in pursuing a personal strategy that leaves no room for error. Adjusting your risk strategy and associated risk threshold to match your specific situation is vital.

In trying to refine my approach to risk I first reflected on experiences from my Naval career and gravitated towards the most challenging ones. This was in part because with no guidance on what was appropriate to my future (aside from the military) I thought of events which gave me the most confidence in my abilities. This is akin to a psychological insurance policy whereby one believes anything can be achieved when a clear goal is not forthcoming.

Using other techniques already discussed I narrowed my desires as follows; self-employment, fulfilment through helping others and complete flexibility as to where I could live (in the context of the previous two requirements). Taking these three points as a guide I concluded that a solid financial base with no unsecured debt, a strong network and a flexible business model would be essential.

When taken together as a combined package, the individual risks inherent in these activities combine to place me in my current situation. Building a strong financial base means saving money or making some informed investments, both of which mean money is allocated and cannot be used for other opportunities. There is also the possibility of complete investment failure. Building a network takes time and energy which could be otherwise spent applying for a full-time professional role. Finding the business model inevitably leads to test and adjustment and the business I now run looks quite different to the one I sketched out a number of years previously.

The opposite of the above is also true. Were I heavily committed financially, or had I started a family, my approach might be somewhat different and there is no "right" answer. Instead by taking the best of your previous experiences and balancing these against the reality of your new lifestyle you can optimise your approach. This will help you to focus only on those activities which add value.

Try to limit external influences on your perception of risk. Advice is valuable but remember that those offering it may have faced very different risks when they were in what they now perceive to be a similar position to you. Listen carefully, analyse slowly and above all only act on things which will help. By doing so you will bolster your individual approach to risk and protect yourself from unforeseen pitfalls.

4 THE JOB MARKET: HUNT, COMPETE, ACHIEVE

The decision to leave the military could coincide with your first exposure to the civilian labour market. Your first impressions may be daunting but do not be alarmed. Some familiar norms apply, including selection methods, a required skill set and a need to deliver on your given objectives. The differences on the other hand are extensive. Motivation to employ you will vary from sector to sector and firm to firm. The range of options open to help achieve your aims (and steer your path) also offer much to consider and vary in their conventionality and ease of access.

If the military career structure can be thought of as a tunnel, with entry at one end (joining) and your departure point at the other (leaving the Service), the civilian market can be compared to a wide grassy field. In the tunnel, you can veer left and right but ultimately the walls keep you on a consistent and forward moving path. In the open field, you can go in any direction. You can run faster or slower or go dramatically sideways. You can stand still, and hope you keep your position. Those coming up behind you will move around or over you. In the tunnel, that can happen, but it is harder, takes longer and follows a similar theme (aligned to your specialist trade or individual Service).

The field analogy is helpful because it allows you to visualise flexibility in a new way. It also illustrates the risks of the open job market. In a wide-open field, you can become lost. Planning is an individual endeavour as is finding opportunities and making the most of them. This offers advantages that are often unavailable in a formalised career structure, but with such advantage comes risk. The first step through the metaphorical gate and into the open field will be your *Curriculum Vitae*, or CV.

The CV

Building and refining your CV is a key step and if you are applying for a competitive position, you will be set against people who may have more experience in writing one. This does not mean that you cannot match or exceed their capabilities, but it does require concerted effort. By the time I applied for salaried roles I had ten variations of my CV tailored to different sectors. These all began with one "master version" which detailed my qualifications, experience, skills and interests. There are many organisations offering CV advice tailored to Armed Forces leavers. The following pointers are based solely on my own experience and do not represent advice from one specific group. Instead they are a combination of suggestions, constructive criticism and my own reflections. The first CV I wrote read like a small novel. The finalised versions were succinct, pointed and quick to digest.

Think about the reader. Like the age-old adage "know your enemy" the first stage of any recruiting process can be among the most brutal. This is because like an adversary whom you know very little about the process can be full of surprises, both helpful and unhelpful. In a large organisation, your CV could be one of hundreds sifted by an individual (or increasingly a computer program) in a day. If done by a person (the majority still are) they will normalise the features of a CV that make the sifting task efficient. Certain words will spring out and put the document into the "yes" pile, perhaps before they reach the end of the document. For this reason certain features of the CV need to be very clear, perhaps in bullet points highlighting key themes. In my experience these are more effective than verbose paragraphs. My first attempts were not succinct or to the point. If you can fit the document into two sides, and read it in around three minutes, you have a good start point from which to refine.

Which skills are relevant? I was a helicopter pilot for most of my naval career. Coincidentally, I had little desire to fly commercially outside the military and so applied to non-aviation roles. Nonetheless when applying to these potential employers or clients, I mentioned flying, because I thought they might find it interesting. If I could not link it to a specific skill required for the role, I would stop mentioning it. Working under pressure, processing information and reaching quick, accurate conclusions can be drawn from flying into non-flying tasks. Use of financial instruments, project management tools or managing large teams are harder to explain and justify. I would draw on a more relevant experience to show those skills rather than mentioning my specialisation.

Bluff at your peril. Honesty is vital throughout this process and in the workplace more generally. If you cannot prove a qualification (particularly a degree or higher) either omit it as a formal qualification or explain it at interview. Do not get into a position where you cannot verify a statement. This damages your reputation and credibility (see Chapter Two). It is better to admit you have a skills gap at interview and consider it an area to improve than to tell a lie. If your CV gets you to interview, you are through the first hurdle. If it does not, pick yourself up and try again, but do not resort to being flexible with the truth.

Ordering. My first CV started with a paragraph about myself, a chronological essay about my military experiences, my academic qualifications and then my personal interests. There is no perfect format, but my ordering changed to a more traditional template as follows. Academic credentials, experience, skills and finally interests, all in bullet points. As an ex-military potential employee your unique experiences may shine through more than your academic qualifications, but you should still include them.

Adding value, not completing tasks. A common criticism of my early CV efforts was that they said a lot about tasks that I had completed but less about the value I added along the way. Phrases such as "delivered an exercise plan involving 100 people and £100m of aircraft" sound good but miss the true worth of what you were doing. Another way pf phrasing that task might be "delivered a major exercise by fulfilling the roles of 3 managers to maximise efficiency". Better still would be a tangible financial figure that you either saved the organisation or a process that you sped up, thereby reducing cost.

This is difficult for all employees to master and potentially even more challenging for a military leaver. All of your activities will have come at a cost to the taxpayer but it is a cost you may have no appreciation of. The military focusses you on your tasks and unless you have worked in procurement or very senior leadership roles you may have had no idea of the significant budgets surrounding your activity. Businesses need people who can find faster and more efficient ways of doing things. It both saves them money and gives them more time to create sales opportunities, converting potential leads into tangible revenue. Try to translate your activities into this context, even if you are very junior in rank. Finding efficiencies that delivered results are translatable achievements that say more about the value you added and less about what you physically did to add that value.

How does the document look? Think about the corporate branding and colours used in the firm you are applying to and consider subtle changes to your document to match. For example, if you are applying to an investment bank with blue livery, maybe use a thin blue border on the document and matching blue title text. This adds to the normalisation of you as a prospect to the recruiter and appeals to sub-conscious norms. It might only add a percentage point to your chances of success, but that might be the final piece of the puzzle. Think about the font you use and how you lay out the document. Do not try to be elaborate. Make the text clear and the message obvious.

Take all advice. As mentioned previously, listen to the advice that adds value and filter that which you cannot resolve or find value in. There are many organisations and individuals who will review your CV. Mine went to my family, colleagues and employers. Accept what feels like harsh criticism. Much of it will improve the document and it will take many versions before it is optimised for wider distribution.

Translating your skills

It is a useful exercise to reflect upon your military roles and try to re-align them to the civilian workplace. Making your experiences relatable to someone who has never served takes time and careful thought. Imagine you are reading the CV of someone from television and film production. Unless you coincidentally have a specific interest in the industry you may struggle to understand the technical terms, industry lexicon and three-letter-acronyms that are normal to those operating on a film set. Take the same principle and apply it to your situation.

How might an investment banker, a manufacturing expert or the manager of a building firm translate your skills into their specific industry? We can assume that unless applying for very specific technical roles you will have limited industry knowledge. The challenge then is to lead the interviewer, CV reader or assessor to conclude that what you have done in some way fits with the specific skills they are looking for. The same can be said in business when trying to sell a product or service. The salesperson, consultant or advisor wants the client to conclude that the product on offer is the solution to their problem.

I will list some examples of military rank ranges and likely skills that could be inferred as a result. The CV reader or interviewer may not know what a "Brigade Operations Officer" or "Executive Warrant Officer" does, but the skills required to execute those duties are relevant in a wide range of situations. I cannot list every role you may have served in, but I will try to group together common themes which you can then expand on in your own research. I use the term "non-technically qualified" to mean those who do not hold specific professional qualifications, such as a commercial pilots' license, membership or a professional body or chartered status. The same "non-qualified" term could apply to a technically qualified individual applying to a new industry, such as a fighter pilot applying to be a mortgage broker:

Junior Officer, non-technically qualified, any Service: Management of small corporate teams, complex problem solving, negotiation between hierarchical stakeholders, project management, determination in the face of challenge, appraisal writing and evaluation, delegation in a resource constrained environment.

Senior NCO, non-technically qualified, any Service: A similar approach in a corporate environment to the junior officer. Potential to highlight experience in certain areas, particularly if qualified in project management related activity.

Junior NCO, non-technically qualified, any Service: Management of individuals in task-critical environments, delegation where appropriate, analysis of risk under pressure, time-management and personal bearing, translating intent into results, being ready to take on greater responsibility at short notice.

Senior Officer, any Service: Strategic decision making within a hierarchy, cross-department collaboration (between mixed teams), industry engagement outside one's comfort zone, international working, budgeting, delegation across corporate functions.

Taking the structure of the company you are applying to and replicating it in your CV to match your skills will also help. For example, when I worked in an operations office I equated it to a Senior Associate or junior Vice-President position in a bank. As such, my CV would show this period of my employment as "VP Operations, XXX Air Squadron".

There are a host of other examples like this. I recently spoke with an officer who had worked as a military assistant to a much more senior individual. He was worried about how, as he put it, "running someone's diary" might look on a CV in the sectors he was applying to. On the contrary, such a role can be very challenging. Managing the diary of the equivalent of a corporate board member brings issues that are very specific to the role but are no less valuable than others. If you feel that you are too junior to apply for a role or underqualified then pause for thought. How might you take your existing experience and show that you can attain greater responsibility? You should aspire to make your rank an irrelevance and instead show how your attitude, aptitude and determination add to your suitability.

Job interviews

Interviews can be daunting, particularly if you have only experienced those required for joining the Armed Forces. To prepare you I will outline some examples of interview questions that you may encounter. The list is not onerous but it is a collection of questions that I have received, that I consider when looking at potential employees or contractors now and that will likely come up in some of your own efforts. I have aimed to make them general so that you can consider them in the context of many roles. As such apply specialist knowledge or expertise to each situation. Research into a business or sector prior to interview will help you understand how questions like this might apply specifically to the role in question. This should give you the best chance of tailoring your response to match.

What made you want to apply for this role?

This type of question seems obvious but you would be surprised how many people apply for jobs and then can't give a short, logical response when directly asked about their reasoning. Have a clear idea about why you want to join an organisation before you walk in.

Tell me about yourself.

This is an opportunity to show your human side while linking parts of your personality to the role or business you are interviewing for. While not always essential, it demonstrates investment in your next career move and provides an opportunity to highlight role specific characteristics that you possess. For example, if you are applying for a customer facing sales role and say that in your spare time you enjoy solitude and being away from people, the interviewer might question your suitability. How will they justify recruiting you to their managers if your role is to win business and deal directly with clients? Consider your future role in the context of your personality traits in this instance.

What are your goals in our organisation?

Before going into the interview room, and preferably before applying for a role, think about the medium and long-term goals you would have should you stay with the business. It is useful to make these specific. For example; "within two years

I want to be the assistant head of my business area by doing the following…. in five years I aim to complete professional accreditation and run my department….in ten years I hope to be a senior partner". This plan will require adjustment depending on the industry in question. Similarly, if your aim is to work somewhere for the shortest time possible it will shine through when you are compared to applicants who believe in the business long-term. Be prepared for this to be pointed out to you if your motivations with a given business have a shorter horizon.

<u>Do you see yourself as a leader?</u>

This question will offer an opportunity to shine but if the answer is rushed the opposite could also occur. Remember, businesses do not practice leadership for the sake of showing that they understand it. The function of leadership (linked closely to management) is used in the way best suited to creating wealth for the business. If having a distinct leadership structure does not support this, then a business may look for a "flatter" and more meritocratic setup. Think about the rigid structures in a large formation in comparison to the smaller and more nimble structures of small military teams. This is the military version of the same principle.

Here, put your leadership experience into context even if you occupied the most junior of ranks in the military. You still have to lead yourself – to get up, look smart, think independently. Some military leavers make the mistake of using leadership as a shield to hide their lack of knowledge about commercial process. Being a great leader in the Roman or Nelsonian sense is impressive, but a more effective approach would be to combine this with an understanding of commercial process in your chosen sector. As such, respond honestly and do not over state your previous leadership credentials. Instead, complement them with industry specific considerations through research and wider reading.

How do you deal with internal conflict?

This question relates to your leadership and personal style. Many of the people you will work with in commercial organisations will not cope well with dogmatic instruction. There will always be a time and a place for more aggressive and forthright approaches but commercial situations are far more nuanced than that. Think about your emotional intelligence in your answer to this question. Showing humility and being able to listen will be of far more use to the wider business than making enemies. Remember, the business has to generate profit to survive and to do so it needs people to work effectively together. This means minimising time spent in conflict with colleagues and retaining key staff, not alienating them or worsening friction. You are unlikely to have dealt with Trade Unions before and this could be a key consideration, particularly if you are applying for a management position. In all cases a business needs people who can bring each other along regardless of surface level tension.

Would you do anything to turn a profit?

This question, or variations of it ("how important is money to you? Do you believe in success at all costs?") is designed to let you show where your moral compass points to and where your boundaries are. Other than the most unscrupulous businesses, most organisations will expect you to operate under a basic personal moral code and also to fall in line with their policies on corporate social responsibility. This means that statements which suggest you would do anything for monetary gain will be a warning sign to employers. They will interpret it as a willingness to be dishonest or take unnecessary risk which will cost them more in the long term than you gain for the business in the short term.

Balance your commitment to commercial gain against your core beliefs in this instance. Is there a disconnect? Are there business activities in your chosen sector that you know you will find difficult to reconcile? Understanding these considerations before any application will help.

You make a mistake that could cost you your position. Would you admit to it?

The answer the interviewer is looking for seems obvious, but the way you answer the question says a lot about your view of integrity, learning and organisational change.

Many of you will have been exposed to a safety culture in the military whereby you are expected to admit to honest mistakes so that others may learn. I recommend that you treat your future role the same way. Hiding behind errors might protect you in the short-term but such errors compound only to be discovered later. This can cause irreparable damage to your reputation in a very short timeframe. The wider detriment to your network and prospects will far outweigh the benefit of hiding the original mistake.

Admit to errors and face the short-term consequences of honest mishaps. At interview you can link this directly to company success; your mistake might cost a small amount in the short term but admitting to it and changing processes might save the company a huge amount in the long-term. This level of insight reflects well on your character and makes commercial sense.

What do you see as the key to the success of the company in the marketplace?

An answer to this question will show how much research you have conducted prior to the interview and how interested you are in the given industry. You will not be expected to have a detailed answer outlining every aspect of the firm and it's competition, but a solid grounding in industry trends and current affairs will help.

With any question relating to the specifics of the business, think about adding your thoughts on future growth potential or strategies. You may be asked about this regardless. Showing that you have given this consideration will likely bode well and suggest that you have a long-term plan to stay with a given company. Recruiting and employing you comes at a cost as does replacing you at short notice. Anything you can do to suggest a positive return on your employment will be viewed positively.

What has been your exposure to diversity and inclusion issues?

Some of you will have worked in male only units or in those where your colleagues fit into a narrow social profile. As a result, some firms will want to assure themselves that you will be comfortable working with more varied groups of people.

It should be noted here that diverse workforces are proven to be more productive and responsive to dynamic change than those that are not. The result is a more effective business. This is one of the reasons why the military goes to great lengths to promote varied recruitment and attempts to break previously held stereotypes surrounding the typical Armed Forces recruit. Private companies and other government bodies are going through a similar change, recognising that diversity of thought adds value. Be honest if in your career you have had limited exposure to people from different cultures, backgrounds or genders. If this is likely to be a problem for you, think long and hard about why that is and address any of your own biases. Holding prejudices is not only morally questionable but it might prevent you from maximising your future opportunities.

<u>*Does your employer know you are here at interview?*</u>

This is another test of your integrity. This question is common across industries, where workers will use a number of methods to avoid telling their current employer that they are interviewing with a competitor. For the interviewing firm, this presents a paradox. They could have the ideal candidate, but that same candidate may have been willing to lie to their current firm to attend the interview. How might they then behave if hired into the organisation? Can they be fully trusted?

As a military leaver it is well understood by many large firms that you can take time off towards the end of your career for interviews and short internships. If an interviewer is unaware of this, simply explain that you are there with the knowledge and support of your current employer. If this is not the case and you are away during a working day with no leave, then you are breaching the contract of your military employment.

We have three candidates and one position to offer. Why should we select you?

A question like this can catch many off-guard, because it presents a risk of appearing arrogant and narcissistic. The key is to communicate your abilities while not being disparaging to the competition.

Focus on your positive attributes and keep any comparison to others generic. If you have a particular strength highlight it here and point out that compared to many other potential employees you are offering a wide range of skills and abilities (if appropriate and true). Think about the role you are interviewing for. What makes you different? How will you deliver value more quickly and consistently than others in this area? Perhaps your qualifications and experience make you a "safe pair of hands" for the role, which means you can sell yourself as a lower risk investment for the company. This is a more effective argument than simply claiming to be capable of doing more good work than other candidates.

Whatever your strategy, avoid down-playing other potential colleagues or making it personal if you happen to know the other candidates. You may both be offered a role at different times and work together. If the manager who is interviewing you sees that you are combative or keen to play down your competition, it may put them in a difficult position should you both be hired. This will equally make it harder for you to build rapport both with your manager and your future team. They may note that you are willing to be rude about others to further your cause. In turn this may mean you are viewed with suspicion. My business partner holds true to the mantra that we should never criticise the competition, we should simply offer a superior service. I wholeheartedly agree and you can apply the same principle to yourself.

Recruiters and agencies

My first port of call when searching for a role was specialist military recruitment groups. I had a good experience with all of them (The List and The White Ensign Association being particularly helpful in my case). These are military specific groups, sometimes run as charities. Your re-settlement adviser is best placed to steer you to those which are optimised for your situation.

Should you seek work through a third-party recruitment firm, an understanding of their business model can help you chose the right one. Like any business, a recruitment agency is selling a product (in this case, you). Getting you to interview might come with a commission, as might finding you a role. This can range from a one-off fee between your new employer and the agency, an on-going retainer whereby employers pay agencies monthly for a constant throughput of staff, or even a percentage of your salary (this is pre-arranged). Recruitment agencies will be keen to have you on their books. The more generic recruiters work on volume of candidates placed and as a military leaver you possess a sound foundation for numerous roles. Consequently, do not be flattered by a keen recruiter or expect the guarantee of a job. Stay composed and focussed no matter how many offers seem to come your way. Remember, there is a significant difference between being brought forward to interview and being offered a position on agreeable terms. Treat every opportunity with the same level of effort and diligence.

Internships

Organised military intern schemes have grown in popularity. When I was leaving, there was a perception in some quarters that these were suited only to former officers, but this is not true. I know a number of successful management consultants and financiers who came from the ranks. It was their drive and hunger for learning that put them into those firms, not their stripes or badges. As such, I recommend that you consider the schemes on offer.

Some internships are paid while others are designed to work around your re-settlement leave and as such are unpaid. Both models have advantages and their suitability will depend on your circumstances. I was reluctant to use my re-settlement leave for an internship, as I saw this as networking and interview time lost. Had I used all of my leave on one firm, and not liked it or failed, my options would have been limited. I would also have lost a lot of valuable time while I was still earning a military salary. Not many industries will pay you whilst you openly search for a new role for weeks, so do not waste this time.

An internship should be treated like any new position and links directly back to your reputation. It can be compared to an extended job interview where both you and your future employer get the chance to know each other. A willingness to commit to anything you are given should shine through. Remember, in a private organisation, your salary represents a cost to the business and what you generate must exceed that cost to make employing you worthwhile. There will be occasions where this does not happen. You might be part of a business strategy that isn't working, or in a firm that has a cash-flow problem. Assume that proving your worth to the organisation is required in order to remain employed long-term. During a down-turn when cut backs are required a firm is more likely to keep those staff it knows it can rely on.

During the early stages in any role it is unlikely that you will be exposed to this but if you are effective quickly, you might find yourself thrust forward sooner than expected.

Informal work experience

This approach can be useful with smaller companies or when your networking activities lead to offers of assistance. Many companies will not have a formal military intern option or they will be too small to offer a scheme bespoke to your skill set and situation. This does not prevent you creating opportunity with them. The following attributes will maximise your opportunity if offered an informal position.

Respectfulness. Showing respect to any potential employer sounds obvious but, in the push to find new opportunity, it can be forgotten. None of your future potential managers (or clients if you aim for self-employment) owe you anything. As such courteous and humble approach is recommended. This will leave most people willing to work with, for, or above you and will leave more doors open should you change course. Small firms thrive on human interaction and showing that you can adapt to this environment will leave employers more comfortable offering you opportunities.

Flexibility. Consider which industries you would be willing to invest time in understanding and the locations they operate in. Would this mean moving home? If you arrange a week of work experience in a new region or country, what are your accommodation and transport options to make the most of the experience? Having a small budget to allow for this is will assist you.

Recording your findings. Treat temporary employment as a fact-finding experience. Document your feelings about the process, including logistical challenges getting to work and where the skill set you are gaining might lead. You will also get a feeling for the structure of the firm, personalities and ethos. Keeping a diary or bullet points in a notebook will help you make informed decisions later.

Who are you competing with?

Your age, ambition and experience will influence where you pitch yourself and what type of jobseeker might apply for the same role. Unless you are applying for work directly related to your military role, it is fair to assume that others will exist who have equivalent or more specific expert knowledge.

A good example might be management consultancy. In my experience many military leavers feel an affiliation with business or management consultancy as a future career. It is perceived by many to be more accessible than technical finance roles while providing excellent learning opportunities and a holistic overview of other industries for new entrants. If applying for such roles you will likely be competing with professionals who have worked in a consulting capacity, speak some of the industry language and have examples of previous relevant experience. Your strategy needs to take this into account and explore ways you can show how you will add value.

Appreciating this dynamic will help you to compete with others. The internet is awash with useful interview tips for specific industries, but if you want an advantage you should try to think as though you were already part of that industry. In the case of management consultancy, many firms publish open source free material on a weekly and monthly basis highlighting their latest thinking on numerous issues (mergers, the internet of things, fintech, recruitment and retention). Try to understand the trends which your chosen industry is focussing on using these resources as a guide. Having some examples pre-researched is also useful. Is there a significant media article that you could analyse and create your own commentary on? Has a major company just announced job cuts or re-structuring? Why might they have done this? These activities might seem laborious and trivial, but they are an interactive way to build industry knowledge and become comfortable with sector specific terms. "Verticals", "balance sheets" and "debt to equity ratio" might sound strange now, but for relevant employers an understanding of these and a plethora of other terms before interview will set you apart. Whilst my focus is on management and finance, the same can be said of any business in any industry.

Sophisticated employers will understand that a military career prevents candidates from building certain skill sets and forearms them with others. By showing an awareness of industry terminology and systems you are reducing employer risk when investing in your training and salary. You are also demonstrating the attributes many employers associate with a military career; diligence, preparedness, hard work and ambition.

Setting your strategy

I have used management consultancy as an example because it is a field I focussed on when considering my options. A similar approach can apply to any sector or skill. Find what is available in the public domain, consume the information and develop a strategy for success. This simple mantra will keep you on a path which will eventually succeed. If you have capacity, you can even try this across numerous sectors at once to see which is of most interest. If you attempt this be prepared for significant amounts of work and manage your fatigue. There is little point learning to think like a management consultant if your energy levels are depleted too quickly. This is where your diet, sleep and prioritisation methods will support you.

My strategy involves measuring my inputs to any task or project and analysing the methods which bring the most effective outcomes. As such I use a time-based approach to my learning and development. In a given day I dedicate set periods to learning and protect them. In the case of my military transition this strategy was refined further.

My commute to work in my final military role involved a forty five minute tube ride during which I would read. That allowed ninety minutes of dedicated learning per day. Public transport is not an optimal learning environment but it is more effective than not devoting any time at all. On weekend I would dedicate a further ninety minutes per day to consolidating my findings from the week. Over seven days, this amounts to ten and a half hours of study. This is significant, but it can be debilitating when managing a demanding role and family commitments. The only way to sustain this level of study and work is to eat properly, sleep as best you can and maintain a core level of physical well-being. Experiment to see what is most effective but be prepared to work hard to achieve your aims. The investment in time and energy will reap longer term rewards.

Test yourself

We often fall back to the things we are most comfortable with when presented with difficulty. If you enjoy reading and writing you may be tempted to focus on these areas in your personal development, rather than mathematical analysis or statistics (and vice versa). It is likely that your military role also lends itself to your preferred skills and that you hope for similar requirements in the future.

Despite this, do not ignore those areas which require improvement. A basic grasp of mathematics can assist in many ways when analysing a business problem. The same is true of being able to read and process information quickly. It is unrealistic to excel in all areas but dedicate some time to understanding your weaknesses and consider whether it is worthwhile improving them. Sometimes completing the hardest tasks to an acceptable standard is more useful than excelling elsewhere.

An alternative perspective

A close friend with over 20 years of senior management experience in the corporate aviation industry offers the following words of caution.

In the early 1980s, I was fortunate to be selected for RAF flight crew training, but before 'signing up' concluded that as an 18 year old, the prospect of a 20 year commitment was too much to reconcile and I elected instead to proceed to university and then follow the well-trodden path towards a commercial flying career. This decision proved to be somewhat pivotal and ultimately led to a 27 year non-flying career in the corporate aviation industry, over 20 years of which as Managing Director of a private jet and helicopter charter, management and engineering company, operating globally for international corporations, high net worth individuals, celebrities and government departments.

Given my natural affinity towards the military, however, I was always happy to see the company receive applications from former servicemen/ women for Flight crew, Ops and Engineering positions. I believed that such individuals would be well trained, disciplined and adaptable to the ever-changing demands of our business.

We set the highest standards for flight operations and, with a high profile and demanding customer base, it was essential that we could rely on our crews, ops teams and engineers to operate to these standards reliably and consistently, regardless of the inevitable challenges that would arise in a dynamic operating environment.

I am pleased to report that the majority of our employment decisions in respect of ex-service personnel were entirely validated by their professionalism, dedication and loyalty to the company; there were of course a few notable exceptions!

At interview we occasionally encountered a mind-set of 'entitlement', particularly from former officers, typically in the form of a "You do of course recognise my previous seniority?" attitude. I believe this may stem, to some extent, from the narrative that former officers who become recruiters may be positively inclined towards employing ex-officer applicants. Whether or not that is true, in the case of civilian recruiters, this approach has very little to commend it.

We occasionally interviewed former Officers who, despite entering the civilian job market for the first time, seemed to genuinely believe that their military rank and experience somehow entitled them to an automatic rite of passage, a seamless move into a civilian role of equivalent standing - **WRONG!**

Although specialist skill sets, qualifications and experience will always be appealing to an employer in certain cases, particularly where candidates possessing such qualifications may be in short supply, this should not be interpreted as a guarantee of success. As a mentor often reminded me, "skills can be taught and qualifications can be achieved, but arrogance and a bad attitude can never be changed."

Even in a small-medium sized business, time in post is essential to enable senior management to assess whether a new addition to the team is settling in and bringing added value in what will be a very different civilian environment with unfamiliar demands and challenges.

Previous military experience may often have little relevance to a civilian role and a former officer who believes he/she can expect or even demand immediate recognition of their previous rank when seeking employment in a commercial business will generally be the recipient of a very unpleasant surprise!

By way of illustration we were, on one occasion, recruiting a Senior Manager for our Ops Team. We interviewed a number of excellent, well qualified and experienced candidates including two former RAF personnel, an ex-Senior NCO and a former Squadron Leader. Coincidentally, they were scheduled for interview consecutively on the same day and met briefly for the first time in our Reception before the interviews began. This fleeting event was later to become pertinent.

As I consistently remind my 16 year-old son, it is essential in life to be self-confident and equally vital to NOT be arrogant; the secret is identifying the location of the thin line between the two.

In the case of our recruitment scenario, both individuals possessed relevant skill sets, although the SNCO had more recent and directly applicable experience. The chasm that existed between the two candidates came, however, in the form of their presentation. The SNCO was self-confident, clearly assured of his competence, but equally respectful of the interview panel and acutely aware that he was potentially entering an unfamiliar world with new operating practices and procedures that he was clearly willing to learn and embrace.

In stark contrast, the former Squadron Leader had clearly forgotten where to "draw the line", or indeed whether a line existed in the first place. Possessing a distinct air of self-importance, he proceeded to present himself as the answer to all of our Operations management aspirations. Despite his lack of recent relevant experience for the position and more importantly his poor preparation and dearth of knowledge of our industry, he nonetheless considered himself to be a potentially 'transformational' addition to our management team and one that we would be crazy to overlook. Sadly for him, we did not require the type of transformation he was offering!

The most incredible element of this story was, however, yet to unfold. A few days after we had written to all candidates and offered the position to the former SNCO, I received a call from the ex-Squadron Leader who had received his letter and, perfectly reasonably, was requesting some feedback on his recent interview. I endeavoured to tactfully deliver some relevant guidance as to how his technique could have been improved and suggested areas to focus on if he was applying for similar positions in the future. His response was astonishing; far from receiving the feedback in a positive and constructive manner, he persisted with his delusion that we had clearly overlooked his 'unique' talents and that we would regret our decision not to offer him the position. He concluded by stating that he sincerely hoped we hadn't offered the post to the 'Flight Sergeant' he had met in our Reception, who clearly wasn't of equivalent calibre!

That particular employment decision was one of the best we ever made, for two very different reasons..!

Change is often positive

This chapter has focussed on positioning yourself to compete with those in industries that are unfamiliar. This assumes a change in career direction but for many this will not be the case. If moving into a related field, the need to spend hours learning the new structures and language of your chosen area may be less pressing. Nonetheless I would still recommend checking that you are as up to date as you can be in your specific field.

In a familiar role you may already possess significant levels of specialist knowledge, referred to in academia as Expert knowledge. This knowledge, which in turn leads to influence, can be very powerful if used correctly. By possessing expertise in specialist areas your value to a related business is more obvious. A generalist approach may leave you with more employment options, but with fewer expert credentials, or more to do as you increase your knowledge across a broader area. An ex-Army friend of mine who has been very successful in the private sector often talks of being "one inch deep" across a wide variety of skill areas. This approach is effective in some instances but be prepared to specialise as your path becomes clearer.

Specialising doesn't have to close doors to future alternatives. In the case of engineering you may broaden into project and programme management, or sales, having never expected to. In order to progress within a business, a willingness to branch out into other areas and take managed risk where others remain in their comfort zone will build your reputation. Consequently this will enable you to command a higher future salary or fee. There is a danger of spreading too thinly and a decision to broaden should be monitored and controlled. This is an area where I took the most advice during my transition to the private sector. When I began my initial research I looked far and wide across a range of industries and employment models. Many of these ideas did not progress beyond my notebook, but I gave them all serious internal consideration and in a few cases met with members of the industry informally to learn more. One of the most enjoyable parts of this process was learning about how people from a completely new professional background were motivated and where their ambitions were focussed. This helped me to question my own motivation and goals, even if the result was a decision not to devote more research effort to that sector or industry.

5 NEGOTIATE, NEGOTIATE, NEGOTIATE

When studying business theory during transition I found the art of negotiation to be among the most interesting. We negotiate daily – with our partners, estate agents, car dealerships. Understanding the value of your skills, and as a result the value you can command from an employer (salary, benefits, time) is nuanced and requires a deep understanding of your chosen industry.

Some of the harshest lessons I learned in my departure from the military involved negotiation in a commercial context. On setting up my business I found myself exposed to real and important negotiations very quickly and with much a stake. I was lucky to have a business partner with extensive experience in negotiating highly complex deals. Success meant a better deal for our business and making the most of the money we had invested. In the early stages these negotiations focussed on our setup as we began renting significant office space, buying equipment and funding research to develop products and services. This evolved into price negotiation whereby we sought to protect the value inherent in our products. While stressful it was also fascinating and I learnt much about when to be patient and when not press for a swift conclusion.

Negotiation comes in many forms and one of the most common

techniques used is anchoring.[4] Put simply, anchoring is the practice of suggesting a figure or action as a start point to "set the scene" for subsequent bargaining. It gives a reference from which you can adjust your position to get the deal you want. Let us consider a hypothetical example. You go to a restaurant and are presented with three wine options. One is £15.99, another is £19.99, and a third is £29.99. The descriptions of the wine are general, you are not a wine expert and the "house" red is the least expensive. You are with someone you are hoping to impress. What do you do?

In this case, the restaurant is trying to anchor you. They hope that you will want to avoid the least expensive wine for fear of looking a little cheap but accept that you cannot justify spending nearly £30. By presenting you the £19.99 wine, they offer you an easy way out. The price is framed by two alternatives. Add to this the likelihood that you are unlikely to have expert wine knowledge, and you select the £19.99 option. What you do not know is that the £19.99 wine is actually the least expensive at wholesale price for the restaurant. When you buy it their profit margin per bottle in percentage terms is a lot more than the inexpensive option and slightly more than the £30 bottle.

In this instance the layout of the wine list has anchored you at a price range where the middle option "looks" most appealing. Your alternatives are to spend more, look like you are counting your pennies in front of your guest, or not drink wine at all. To some these alternatives are perfectly acceptable, but to most they are not. The restaurant is planning for this through their market research and experience. They have also assessed the likelihood of you spotting a quality difference in the taste of the wine to be low.

Let us apply this model to salary negotiation. Remember that with the exception of any specific extra allowances based on your role, your basic salary as a member of the military is available to view online. Add to this the fact that many major ex-military transition schemes are run by ex-military managers, and it is hard to disguise your previous earnings. Employers can therefore easily familiarise themselves with what they think your expectations might be. This is also true if you have a military pension or other income that is known to those interviewing you.

In this instance I recommend that you value your skills based on the company size and structure, rather than having a pre-determined view based on your military salary. We all have a minimum figure below which we cannot maintain our core living standards, or below which we are unwilling to dip in the pursuit of our goals. Hold this in reserve as your "no lower than" figure. Then, consider the fact that your employer will have a "no higher than" figure for your salary. Some will be openly negotiable on this whereas others may take a hard line early on. If dealing with a firm that refuses to negotiate salary, think carefully before questioning their logic. The business has been honest with you form the outset so you may need a compelling reason before disputing this statement and asking for more.

Let us assume that you have latitude to negotiate your benefits. These are not confined to money, and you should consider them in the context of your long-term objectives. Shares, extra holidays, a car or a private health insurance package can offer tax-efficient and capacity saving benefits that an increase in salary (or bonus) may not. Also, exercise caution when attempting to increase bonus offers. These are often performance related, both on you and the wider business and are rarely easily won. Never assume that because you successfully negotiate a better bonus offer you will achieve it.

Salary offers should be treated with discretion and not discussed with other potential colleagues or job applicants. Your offer should be considered an individual one based on your value proposition as an employee. Understanding the financial health of a company before going to interview may assist you in pitching your negotiation levels. Ultimately, a firm will view you as an individual risk and this should be considered when challenging any offer.

In many companies, particularly in sales or business development roles, you will be expected to go out and win clients, conclude deals and increase revenue. This will require you to assess the likelihood of success and to negotiate in a way that keeps clients interested but does not over emphasise the point, while remaining convincing. If you aren't willing to do this for your own salary, will you have the appetite for it when selling the product? There is no hard and fast rule here, but politely challenging the first salary offer and justifying your position can show determination, articulateness and intelligence, if done well. If done badly, it can reflect very poorly on your character, which in turn damages your reputation. It is up to you to assess this situation based on the employer, the strength of your skill set and your desire to succeed and take the position. As with many of the subjects discussed in this book there is no time wasted in preparation, so work to understand these factors before walking into an interview.

Know when to stop

There is something addictive about negotiating. Once you start, there is a risk that this feeling starts to overtake your end goal. I suffered from this a number of years ago when trying to buy my first house. I searched for over eighteen months and viewed over fifty properties around South-West England. I was between deployments and so had a narrow time frame to make decisions and was quite badly placed to negotiate. I had not applied for a mortgage before and had limited time to conduct viewings. My initial offers were usually quite low (partly due to the fact that I didn't have any experience in how to assess the true value of a house) and I rarely reached a point where I offered anywhere near the asking price.

Eventually I bought a house for somewhat more than the asking price and renovated it. This proved to be a good decision and allowed me to grow my confidence in the field of property purchase. At the time however I was unsure about whether my decision was correct. This self-doubt proved to be healthy and I thought back to some of the other properties I had viewed. There were other properties I could have bought and made a small profit on before settling on my final choice. The lesson was that if you can see value in something where others do not, quantify that value and pursue it.

The same can be said of other negotiations. You may have a view of your self-worth, based on internet research, friends in the industry, or simply a straightforward belief that you should earn

X an hour, day or month. As you cast your search wider this figure will change as you receive positive and negative feedback. Your negotiating strategy should change with it.

As you begin to understand your value to a business (including potentially your own), tempter your negotiation to those opportunities that will offer a realistic chance of success. In the early stages of your transition you will have time to experiment with this but as the critical moment comes when your military salary stops, you need to be surgical in your approaches to achieve success. By refining your strategy you will both grow in confidence and appear more credible to future employers and clients.

Humility and the paradox of experience

There is a tendency for some service leavers to appear arrogant when approaching employers or clients. On rare occasions it is linked to a deep sense of entitlement. In more nuanced terms it masks insecurity created by the uncertainty of a drastic career change. I call this "the paradox of experience".

Military structures in the West exist as they after centuries of strategic and tactical evolution. While imperfect they still offer a predictable yet flexible framework around which dynamic decision making can take place under pressurised and unique circumstances. The hierarchical structures still used in the UK Armed Forces are replicated across NATO and further afield for good reason.

Whereas the nature of conflict is changing rapidly, the rate of change is pedestrian compared to the ways technology is changing the workplace. The result is that many military leavers, particularly those who have served for extended periods, find a labour market that is completely different to the one they interacted with before joining.

For a more experienced candidate an assumption that they can match their salary or seniority in a new organisation is increasingly flawed when viewed through a modern labour market lens. In this instance, specialising is the most likely route to salary matching or rapid progression. In a more general role the negotiating position of such a candidate is initially weak and leads many in this situation to join other large institutions with similar hierarchies. The risk for these candidates is balanced by the likelihood that they have an immediate pension on leaving the military.

Should you be such a candidate there are very lucrative offers from large businesses whose pension plans and benefits packages are comparable to the Armed Forces. I counsel you to consider your value to the new business before expecting too much. This value can be added early by dedicated study in your chosen field or increased work experience. Firms like this are often located in large cities, although many have located supporting parts of the business outside London offering more geographical choice.

Conversely, smaller firms will likely offer the chance for faster career progression, personal fulfilment and a much more personal business learning experience. This comes with the likelihood of a reduced initial salary and benefits package. As a result negotiating with small companies like this has to be realistic.

Consider your long-term growth and how you feel working in an institution such as the military. If you enjoy the scale and stability, then the larger firms may offer the right balance in your new career. If seeking agility at the cost of short-term benefits and job security, look at smaller businesses in sectors with high predicted growth. Whichever you choose, adjusting your negotiating style to match could pay dividends.

Communicate to influence

Communication is an area of study and activity that the military is well accustomed to. Despite this, the science behind effective interpersonal communication is often overlooked. In this section we will examine the science of communication and how it alters your ability to influence others. We will discuss communication and influence in the context of negotiation but the lessons identified can be used anywhere. These methods are particularly applicable to situations where you are managing people, or being managed yourself.

We communicate to achieve and end-state, to exert influence on others such that they carry out a task in support of an organisation or our own interests. This book is an example. In reading it, I hope to influence your thinking in a way which optimises your transition to civilian employment and as a result see you recommend this book to friends and colleagues.

To influence others effectively we must fully understand the tools at our disposal. For this I will refer to Soft, Hard and Rational influence techniques[5]. These alter the way we communicate to achieve both simple and complex aims. Let us consider each in turn.

Hard

These techniques are those commonly used in basic military training. They are directive, sometimes aggressive and make very clear that the communicator wants you to do something because they have the authority to demand it. This might conjure images of a Senior NCO on a parade square but these methods are not restricted to the obvious approach. The use of threats and an invasion of personal space also fall into this area and it is a common perception that Hard influence techniques are often negative.

This is not so. Hard techniques have a place must be used sparingly if they are to be effective. Think of a time when a more senior manager or colleague has reacted angrily to a minor mistake in a public or group setting. Such a rection damages the ability of that individual to use these techniques when the need is urgent. In order to remain effective this level of chastisement should be used in context and when an urgent result is needed.

There are many examples of individuals in positions of authority, when removed from their comfort zone, reacting angrily to subordinates for seemingly minor misdemeanours where coaching and assistance is required. Similarly, there are times when Hard influence is necessary and managers are reluctant to use the techniques, perhaps due to over-familiarity. The method relies on escalation which means one must not start with such a directive technique unless absolutely necessary.

Hard influence techniques come in many forms. Pressure, assertiveness and the use of management coalitions to force and action by a subordinate party may be familiar to you. Legitimating is another. This is the use of a position to garner compliance from another party, colloquially known both inside and outside the military as "pulling rank". Exchange is a technique that I did not experience often during my military career but is worthy of note in a commercial context. This is the act of offering to "do someone a favour" at a present or future point in exchange for immediate compliance. This technique is often used where a conflict of interest is developing on a project or where a manager wished to diffuse a potential situation that may arise in the future.

Judicious use of these influence techniques could pay dividends when there is intense time pressure or a need to achieve an aim with limited scope for deviation. Examples include a well understood problem which is recurrent or an unexpected problem where time spent in deliberation results in high cost. Hard techniques are by no means the most effective in terms of team commitment and repeated use with a team may lead to alienation and disenfranchisement. Escalate appropriately or use such techniques when the situation demands it for optimum results.

Soft

These techniques are common to both the public sector and commercial environment. Sometimes characterised as "pull" tactics, they aim to encourage personal investment in a task and in doing so achieve longer-term commitment. While this is often beneficial to both the individual and the organisation concerned, commitment can take longer to achieve. As such if a task is time critical soft influence techniques may not be the optimum solution.

Soft influence techniques take many forms and it is likely that you use some of them already. Ingratiation involves offering personal praise or positive comment prior to asking an individual to complete a task. Personal appeal is another tactic which relies on an existing relationship. The loyalty that results leads to a desire to help when requested.

Inspirational appeal is a variation on personal appeal, where a manager or peer can appeal to individual values and emotions to achieve compliance. This may not rely on an existing relationship but it requires the manager in question to understand the core values of the team. Military leadership features inspirational appeal on many levels, from junior NCO through to Heads of Service. This type of leadership is effective in the military because core values are well defined and instilled throughout the recruitment and training process.

Consultation involves giving some choice to the individual who will be asked to comply or risk losing a privilege. For example, as a manager you may need to ask a team member to give up leave to complete a critical task. In order to soften the request you offer them choice as to when this time is taken from the diary. This method is also common in the military where restrictive duties must be shared between a team, particularly over public holidays and weekends.

Collaboration is an alternative method. This involves removing obstacles to compliance meaning that a team can commit more easily. For example, a manager who provides their team with access to additional resources would be seen as a collaborator. In the context of a salary negotiation, a number of soft techniques might be used by employer or applicant to achieve a desired end-state. The willingness to negotiate is a function of need. Specialist skills or work in undesirable locations might mean an employer is more willing to negotiate to recruit the right candidate. Similarly, in an industry where there are many applicants, there is less imperative for an employer to meet applicant demands. Consider this in your research prior to beginning your negotiation.

Regardless of your rank, you will have been subject to soft techniques or required to use them to achieve an objective. By developing your understanding of influence theory you can optimise it's use in and protect yourself from it when appropriate.

Rational

This is the use of statistical analysis to reinforce a course of action. It is most effective where data exists and is readily at hand. For example: "You need to open the coffee shop one hour earlier at 0745 as we have found statistics that show the most people get off the bus-stop outside and walk to work between eight and half past".

This technique is often used in conjunction with hard or soft tactics, rather than in isolation. There is a risk of appearing patronising if delivered abruptly or without context. If that data you are using draws obvious conclusions it should be delivered delicately, or be left available for reference if required. In the context of employment, this technique can be useful where data is hard to acquire but finding it successfully shows that you can add value. This could be industry specific statistics or obscure data from an academic journal. Think about a piece of marketing material you have seen where a statistic or graph is used to show how a product has improved the situation of a customer. This is an example of rational influence.

Remember where you started

Regardless of the level you aspire to in an organisation, remember that transferring military skills into the civilian sector is not straight forward. Suggesting dogmatically that military leadership has great application commercially could lead to complacency. It is true that military skills have much to offer in a business context but only with the appropriate level of industry specific knowledge. This viewpoint also unhelpful if you are leaving the military from a place of lower seniority or having not promoted at all. Those of you in this position offer the same value commercially as those more senior provided that value is delivered and new ways of thinking can be embraced. Maintaining your humility and showing that you are ready to learn will stand you in good stead during any negotiation.

6 EDUCATION

I view education as an insurance policy and I have heard the same phrase used countless times by others. Like insurance, education is often not required in the short-term. When a sudden need arises and none is in place the costs can be significant. While qualifications must always be viewed in the context of experience a solid educational base is essential for both personal development and professional success.

Learning is a challenging undertaking, particularly as an adult. It requires diligence and energy and so it is helpful to focus on areas which you have an interest in. What was your learning like at school? Were you a good student, or did you neglect the time available to glean new knowledge? Whatever your previous experience of learning do not let your perceived ability to learn slow you down. When I undertook my first qualification (having joined the Naval Service with A levels) it took time to re-adjust to academic learning. Military methods of teaching do not always support analysis and evaluation, and where they do, it is often in an abstract manner. These methods do however offer a good foundation from which to enhance your future learning, whether re-taking GCSEs or embarking on a PhD.

Consider your stated goals and model your learning plan around them. Education can be about so much more than finding employment. Your mind is a muscle and the more you can test its capabilities the stronger it will become. During my move to civilian self-employment I worked on my commercial pilots' license and business studies courses at the same time and found that these very different areas had some interesting similarities. My maths improved, my ability to process information grew and my confidence in job seeking was enhanced, all through self-study and dedicated learning time.

Education can be expensive. Before paying for a course, consider your options. Would it be sensible to buy a book on the subject in question? This might help you understand it in more detail before committing to a course. Are there funding options through your re-settlement package, or learning credits, that you could use? My initial ambitions started with a desire to learn the intricacies of accountancy, before further reading helped me to understand that I wanted an overview of how large financial systems worked rather than a dedicated financial accounting course. Throughout this process I read textbooks, biographies and completed an online business course. Only then had I truly understood what I wanted to learn. Better still, by expanding my mind and dedicating time the early stages of resettlement, I created capacity in my final months of service. My efforts were then dedicated to business setup and product development.

If you are still unsure as to your preferred educational path, consider short online courses. These are run by leading universities at low cost and can offer you options to explore numerous topics. They are very efficient I that you could enrol in a number at once and tend to last only a few weeks or months. In my case, I completed an Masters in Business Administration certificate.

This course covered the topics of a full MBA over 10 weeks. Whilst in no way equivalent to a full Masters it helped me refine the areas I wanted to understand more deeply. It also introduced me to new areas that I hadn't considered and gave me new perspectives on subjects such as leadership and management, marketing and business operations. The world of business has some compelling leadership examples, where individuals balance enormous personal financial risk against potential reward and convince others to do the same.

On completion of my course I subscribed to online journal feeds from leading consultancies, which in turn, send out supplements and short articles highlighting their work. This body of knowledge slowly built on my initial foundation. I firmly believe that to date my experiences of education, both formal and informal, have proven to be my greatest asset.

Managing your diary to fit learning into your spare time is challenging. It requires high levels of discipline and an unwavering desire to succeed. I have mentioned how I used commuting time to read or make short noted on subjects of interest. Public transport is by no means the ideal learning environment and I would commend you to segregate time and space at home to your own development. A local library or workspace is just as appropriate. Library membership is an enormous asset which, when combined with online open source research, offers an abundance of material on any subject.

Informal education

What is the purpose of education? Is it to build the foundation for experience-based learning? Is it a natural extension of your desire for self-discovery? We all view education differently. It comes with alternative meanings and supports different goals. I know many successful people who have no formal education. Whereas I chose to study while working, my sister dedicated time to the endeavour and is an accomplished academic (she is also younger than me, so year for year, she has made much better use of her time)! Education has been used completely differently by both of us and we have both found very different utility in it. A friend of mine often reminds me how he had no formal education and yet he is one of the most compassionate and capable people I have ever met. His worth is neither increased nor decreased by his educational status, it has just influenced his life and decision making in different ways. He and I would often discuss how some of his customers would treat him based on assumptions about his status. The irony is that those who may chose to judge often have far superior qualifications, but they still seek to do business with him above others.

This is where education should be viewed in context, particularly if you began your military without impressive formal qualifications. Gaining knowledge is important and using that knowledge to either improve your life and wellbeing is very rewarding. You do not need to gain that knowledge on a formal course or in a recognised institution, but it will help with certain roles if you can.

A late friend of my family had followed an intriguing educational path. He left school to move away from the UK having very few formal qualifications. Over the following years and into his twenties he worked as a shipping agent, trained as an RAF pilot, was at sea in the Merchant Navy and then moved into finance. His unique family circumstances took him to Canada as he turned thirty, where he enrolled in a local University to study economics as a mature student. He went on to build a business over many years that made him one of the wealthiest men in Canada. More importantly, he chose to use that wealth to help others. In the final stages of my Naval career he would often suggest that I take time out to study at a formal institution in the way that he did. I have not, but his advice is nonetheless sound and his actions inspire me to press forward with my own business ambitions. Studying full-time may not appeal financially or in practical terms but immersion in a place of dedicated learning has tangible benefits over home study.

If like me you served in countries where education is segregated by wealth, gender, religion or geography you may have noted the impact such a system had on those societies. Consider this when you are debating whether to devote time to self-study. Education is a privilege and one which many of us take for granted.

An Alternative Perspective

Chelsey David has been teaching secondary and adult learners since 2010. A Law graduate of Bristol University, with a Masters from Swansea and a PGCE from the University of Oxford, she now writes for Journals on subjects ranging from Ancient History to Women's Rights. She is a well-respected educational writer and researcher who has kindly offered to give her thoughts on learning as a subject matter expert.

Eleanor Roosevelt, wife of the then US President, once remarked that 'education only ends with death'.[6] This is both heartening and depressing when we consider that school is only the start of what is, in many ways, a life sentence.[7] All adults, whatever their position or profession, will engage in education beyond the age of eighteen. It is a vital aspect of life to grasp as we prepare for shifting and rapid advances in technology and the associated impacts on society and the workplace.[8] My contribution offers guidance your approach to adult education but remember that everyone has individual needs. There is no right or wrong answer save to say that by dismissing education beyond your early years you might miss significant opportunities for personal growth and financial success.

Education for formalised professions

If you wish to enter into a profession there are often non-negotiable educational requirements directly linked to the field in question. For example, if you wish to practice law or medicine you must have a qualifying degree (in law or medicine) followed by a further period of study for a certificate of professional competence that allows you to practice. This process involves several years of study, significant financial investment and initially working for lower rates of pay.

Our education system is in many ways still geared for this template. If a less conventional route appeals there are many professions where a flexible and negotiable approach is fostered. What both routes share is the achievement of a high level of educational attainment. This in turn links to the roles in a given industry, whose high standards allow the term "profession" to be used. Such standards are formalised through the industry entry requirements and ongoing development through a professional body. Consequently, a degree or an apprenticeship scheme often form part of the minimum entry requirements. Examples of professions where this is now the norm include teaching, accountancy, law and medicine. A combination of formal education and experience eventually leads to promotion and credibility in these professions.

In these fields the approach you take can be as important as your formal education. Let us imagine that you wish to qualify a teacher. The profession offers many variations that you may not have considered. For example, a state school would require a degree followed by a certificate of teacher training, either provided through a teaching school or university. This would then be followed by a further year of development in a school proving yourself in role. By contrast a private school may only ask for a 'good degree' and be equally interested in your ability to run an extra-curricular club or sporting activity. As such, doing your research on your desired profession is helpful before taking the plunge into adult education. Work in the early stages could save you time and money. Look at the staff profiles of the businesses where you think you will apply for a role to see if there is a common educational background. Try to determine the educational level that employees in that industry or firm seem to share. Do they have degrees, professional or vocational qualifications? Do firms you are interested in offer in house training and educational programs that allow you to learn and earn? Education can form a part of your employment package in the same way that private health insurance can and as such it may form part of your negotiation strategy.

It should also be noted that professions which do not require a degree will expect you to earn role or sector specific qualifications. Many firms still state a degree requirement in their recruitment literature. Consider the value in applying to these even if you do not have the prerequisite qualifications. Your experiences will be unique and many employers will value those as highly as a degree, if not more so.

Home-based learning

If you decide pursuing a formal qualification to support a job application or self-employment, consider the following factors:

- How long will it take to achieve the qualification?
- How much will it cost?
- What benefits (including enjoyment) will I glean from it?

These three factors have to be weighed up carefully before you embark on a given course of action. For instance, I would very much like to spend a year studying the history of art while living in Italy. I know that doing so, including all living expenses and tuition fees, would cost me in excess of £20,000. It would be of limited benefit to me in terms of my chosen career, require me to take a reduction in salary and also to move my family. As such, I devote my time to other qualifications that are both affordable and of greater value. If I choose to take the risk and do the course, there is a danger that my initial enthusiasm will be replace with a sense of "forced" learning. That is, even though I initially am enthusiastic, the pressure this qualification puts me under in other aspects of my life becomes a driving influence and one which removes any enjoyment. At that point, I would simply be persevering for perceived career benefit and a sense of duty having committed irreversibly to the course.

Pursuing a course of action out of a sense of obligation or third party pressure is known as extrinsic motivation.[9] Research has shown that this can often lead to poorer outcomes in terms of enjoyment, depth of learning and eventual achievement.[10] Simply put, think back to a subject you were forced to study in school but did not enjoy. This feeling of reticence will remain regardless of how long ago that was. This problem worsens when applied not only to your field of study but any follow-on job application or business plan. Not only are you more likely to reach a lower standard of attainment, you will have to appear convincing in an interview for a role with limited appeal. Adult learning can help you understand this dynamic before you reach formal interview.

Once you have chosen your preferred professional field you should assess fully the options that adult education can offer. Two of the most common routes to gaining qualifications are home study or attending a formal institution. As a military leaver you may already have some formal technical or project management qualifications and your approach to adult learning should consider how these might be of best use to you.

Home based learning

Advances in technology make this an appealing option. Gone are the days where you might lock yourself in your home study or bedroom with endless books to work through. The availability of smartphone and portable technology combined with online resources means you can be learning at any time and in any social environment. This is a huge advantage if you have responsibilities with your family or need to support your learning while still serving in a demanding military role.

We learn best when we are in environments that make us feel emotionally and mentally comfortable. This is of critical importance if you are educating yourself after a long break and feel apprehensive about what is required. In your home you have the advantage of being able to make mistakes, experiment and choose exactly when and how you will go about studying.[11]

There are also major logistical advantages. Studying at home can often be a wise financial move as courses are offered at lower rates, you do not need to pay for transport or extra food and you have options to buy, borrow or download course materials as and when required. In recent years Massive Open Online Courses (MOOCs) have enabled learning alongside programmes created by universities, colleges and foundations at very low cost.[12] Courses are provided by some of the world's leading universities and are an excellent way to both re-engage with learning and to try a field you may be less familiar with. MOOCs also have the benefit of adding to your CV quickly. Enrolling shows clear evidence of initiative and a hunger for learning when applying for future study or work. To enrol you only need to have an email account and a means of logging in, eliminating many of the barriers that existed in the past. You can also fit the learning around your non-discretionary commitments such as childcare and current employment, as you can study at your own pace and set your own agenda.

Everyone has different needs and home-based learning offers the flexibility to tailor your experience. You can emphasise your personal interests with the least disruption to existing commitments which should theoretically lead to better learning outcomes. This route to learning has been the preferred choice for adults from all walks of life and of all ages for over twenty years.[13]

In order to make the most of the advantages home based learning offers there are some important considerations. Does your home have a place where you can easily study and focus without distraction? This does not have to be a dedicated study room. In austere conditions around the world many are educated in poor and overcrowded living conditions and still participate in work and learning to the best of their ability. If your home or military accommodation is not your preference is there another location nearby that you can go to, such as a café, library or community centre? Finding a place where you can work for periods without undue distraction, preferably with internet access and the option of light refreshment will aid your learning.

Let us consider some disadvantages of the home-based approach. This method of study can be a solitary experience, particularly if you are used to conducting learning in large groups. Learning has long been proven to have a social dimension.[14] The most valuable and powerful learning experiences often involve sharing our ideas with others and in turn learning from them. The interactions are equally valid whether with our peers or dedicated experts.[15] An aspect of MOOCs worth considering is that should you have refined or in-depth questions you will have limited opportunity to explore these on the course. You could be one of thousands logging in for that particular piece of material or lecture video. While home-based options offer convenience and low cost such a route comes with compromise which may not suit your desired outcomes.

Institution based learning

Learning is a cultural and social experience and it is one that all adults will engage with throughout their lives. [16] Spending time with a recognised expert in a group allows you to learn from both real life experience and abstract theory. This allows the group to identify the advantages and disadvantages of a particular way of thinking or analysis and to share alternative perspectives.[17] Interestingly, experts such as Hasmann argue that through group learning we are able to gain a mastery over skills to a level we would not achieve by ourselves. Similarly, our work with peers and experts allows us to learn 'tricks of the trade' that we would be unlikely to learn alone.[18]

If you engage with an institution to aid your learning it is important to choose a provider who will work with you and for you. Marion Terry, an expert in adult education, points out that a course provider must provide learners with consistent standards and a stable environment. This includes independence, autonomy of choice, the opportunity to take responsibility for one's own learning and opportunities to grow confidence.[19] In addition, options to tailor courses to individual wants and interests will increase the likelihood that you will remain on the course in the long-term. Options for flexible attendance are increasingly common and like flexible working are very popular.[20] The more a course provider cater for these measures the more likely you are to succeed. Do not assume that a well-known name and tradition will provide a great education. Sometimes it will, but often the only certainty is that it will demand very high fees!

It is also important to note that the relationship between tutor and student is a professional one. That means that both sides are expected to conform to certain norms and standards and your initial interactions with the institution will act as an indication of how it treats enrolled students. Contacting individuals as well as the general admissions department is key. It is reasonable to expect that if you get in touch with an individual lecturer or admissions department you will hear back. If you do not, or if the response strikes you as dismissive or awkward, this may be an indicator of the kind of support you will (or will not) receive should you enrol. As such, think carefully before committing financially to any one institution. Use first impressions as a guide to your decision making.

Keep you aims front and centre at this early stage. A supportive tutor or institution can be very helpful in your future job search. This might be through recommending helpful networking events or offering impartial but valuable advice about your options. Some of the best tutors I had would write well-constructed references, answer questions on future career options, lend me materials and even conduct practice interviews. One rather impressive tutor even spent two afternoons a week trying offering me specified extra tuition so that I could reach the top grades. He did this for free, well beyond his contractual obligations. Not everyone will offer this level of support, but it is worth considering how such networks and individuals could support you. They can help you build on your knowledge and skills alongside building your wider professional network.

Institutional learning has disadvantages. Some providers do not allow you to tailor your course content and insist you stick to a pre-designed program. This is especially true in condensed professional courses. Some institutions may be inflexible in terms of attendance and may even require you to reduce your hours in full-time work as part of their entry requirements. Also consider the culture and ethos of an institution in the context of your experiences to date. What kinds of learners do they have? Are they focussed on one age group or demographic? Will you be comfortable in that demographic? How much financial or pastoral support does the institution offer? Are the facilities you will be paying for well-maintained and resourced?

The military is well resourced in terms of internal education and adult learning when compared to many other institutions. Use these facilities in your final year of service to their maximum. Whether funding options, free library access or online material, ensure that you take full advantage of the time and technology at your disposal. As an adult learner leaving the military you have so many options, it may seem difficult to choose right path. My advice is, do not dismiss education as a youthful pursuit. Make a plan that is unique to your situation and stick to it. At the same time think about how continuing your learning might help you become a more rounded individual. Your future career is important but so too is your personal development and wider knowledge. Quite simply, find what you like and do it.

7 NETWORKING

There are many forms of networking. They are not limited to formal events or dedicated personal development activities. Each time you interact with another person you are potentially linking yourself to an opportunity. That is not to suggest that every interaction must focus on business or the desire to secure a role. I am referring to mindset where one seeks out opportunity where none may be obvious. A willingness to show interest on your part might prompt another connection to form and blossom to the point that commercial benefit results. If it does not, you may discover a helpful lead that takes you tangentially to a new opportunity. The utility of a strong network is endless if properly managed.

Building a personal network has no defined pattern and should make best use of your existing resources, whether they are personal connections or access to modern technology. Networking is an art form which can be modified as your transition matures. Like education, it should not stop on achievement of your short term aims. To me, networking is simply finding like-minded people, forming a connection and maintaining it. As a service person dedicated networks are already established to help you. These range from the more obvious, such as military networking groups established on Linkedin, to more subtle approaches which target specific industries. The List is a particularly effective networking group which I implore you to consider as part of your transition planning.

Remote networking, using social media or online services, offers an efficient system for building contacts and establishing links across a broad spectrum of businesses. Particularly for those based in remote locations it may be the only effective option in the early stages. In order to make the most of your online strategy, consider the following pointers when sending messages, particularly when approaching a new contact for the first time.

Understand your requirement. Before sending an online message consider exactly hat you hope to achieve. Are you looking for advice, a link to a specific business, work experience or an interview? Ensure that whatever the purpose of the message it is clear from the outset.

Succinct messaging. When sending a message for the first time, particularly on a business networking site, make it clear that you are seeking advice and not selling a product. These sites are regularly used by sales people and marketing agents to reach out to influential potential customers. By keeping your messages short you both minimise the time a senior executive spends reading it and on opening the message it is less likely to look like a speculative attempt at sales.

Politeness. Ensure that your message beings with a greeting and ends with thanks for the time taken to. I recommend avoiding presumptuous tones. "I look forward to hearing from you" may, to some, appear suggestive that a response is assumed. "Kind regards", "All the best" or "Many thanks for your time" are more deferential and leave the reader with no preconceptions.

Once established in the commercial environment you will find that online networking and speculative messaging is commonplace in some industries. At this early stage, use caution. Only commit statements to writing that you are willing to endorse or justify. This is helpful advice for all written correspondence.

In order to optimise your networking strategy I recommend a combination of remote methods and face to face interaction. Whatever your military background there will be elements of your career that are fascinating to others. In order to convey your character and to maximise your personal impact meeting in person is a must. Body language, tone and bearing can all be conveyed quickly and both parties can attempt to visualise working with the other. I made use of the White Ensign Association and The List, the latter offering regular and well-structured opportunities to meet groups of potential employers.

Do not discount non-military local networking groups. As a service person you may be unique at such events and will likely meet people from your local area. All of these interactions offer opportunities for you to practice the language of business and to refine your personal style.

A partner from a large consultancy once explained that in his field, his network was key to success. Treating your networking plans as a "consultancy project" can be a useful way of approaching the task. Like a consultancy project, it requires thorough planning, energy, diligence and a willingness to take advice. Let us consider these aspects in turn.

Thorough Planning. Take time to meticulously scrutinise your plan to connect with people. Link this to the foundation of your ambition. Which industries will be your focus and where are they concentrated? Do they have a trade show or business event you can attend? Is there a recruitment event you can register interest in? With these questions answered, divide your time between online activity, group networking events and direct approaches to key influencers. Always remain courteous and flexible . For example, if interested in a project management role in the construction industry, seek out those who left the military at a similar level in the same area. Ask them straightforward questions regarding their recruitment and current industry trends. Then write to companies directly stating that you are a service leaver looking to learn more about their business. Better still if you can foster links in the industry contact them directly. In the majority of cases people will find time to help but you will have to make time for them. Assume that their diary takes priority and that you are the one who will change your schedule. Face to face meetings like this are invaluable and will help you to focus effort as your plan matures.

Your polite proactivity will impress many of those you contact, but always leave the door open for them to refuse further contact. For example, "I fully understand if your busy schedule prevents you from responding and appreciate your time nonetheless in considering my message". A sign-off like this leaves the receiver an opportunity to disengage without embarrassment. Importantly, it also allows them to reconnect with you should a future opportunity arise.

Conversely, a message as follows is likely yield a negative reaction from a sophisticated manager or employer.

"Good afternoon.

I am an ex-military operator with significant leadership and command experience. I have served globally and feel I am a good fit for your firm. I would like to meet to discuss job opportunities and potential interview dates. I am available on the 05th, 07th and 09th of May.

I look forward to your response,

J Smith"

In this message the writer is implying that they know as much if not more than the receiver about their industry. This is based on the assumption that the writer feels they would be "a good fit" without further investigation or direct experience. Self-proclaimed leadership qualities as well as an assumption that the receiver will move diary events suggest arrogance and a sense of entitlement.

A considered and humble approach is more likely to succeed. State that while you have useful transferrable skills you are keen to develop your commercial credentials outside the military. Highlight reasons why you are attracted to that industry or specific business (ethos, brand, varied work). Aim to show a willingness to invest your time and energy rather than demand attention.

Energy. Research, correspondence and continued engagement require energy. In the final stages of my military career and as the business was being established I would often work far beyond what would be considered a normal working day. This included making time for a healthy diet and routine exercise. The time required to build on my existing network, as well as develop new connections, was significant. When those you reach out to respond many may request an initial meeting and you may have to use evenings, weekends and annual leave to honour those requests. One meeting will lead to another, friendships could develop and those same connections may start introducing you to colleagues. It might not take long before you find yourself with little remaining capacity and your activities may start to suffer. In this case focus on those connections that you feel offer the greatest chance of developing an opportunity. If it is too early to tell or you feel unsure, follow your instincts.

Diligence. A willingness to persevere even under the most challenging circumstances will allow your network to flourish. This becomes particularly pertinent when maintaining existing relationships. This situation is common in the final months of service where time away from work is still limited but connections have to be kept relevant and appraised of your plans. Judgement is required when maintaining these relationships. Some may be willing to engage regularly and actively seek your time, while others remain cautious. Establishing a frequency to your interactions will demonstrate that you are both sympathetic and considerate of the pressures many of your contacts face. Politely ask whether one meeting a quarter would be acceptable, or perhaps a follow-on meeting in your final months of service. Many connections will be happy to give up their time provided that you remain willing flex around their compressed diaries.

Plan your engagements carefully as you receive responses to requests. Be meticulous and do not compromise on detail with regard to contingency planning. What if the trains are delayed on the day of your travel? Or your car fails to start? The opportunity to engage prior to seeking employment is one to be guarded and allow yourself time to make alternative short-notice plans. In addition to this detailed approach, use automated tools such as calendar reminders to notify you when an interaction is due.

Meeting contacts face to face offers opportunity to connect on a personal level. Show interest and remember personal details that those you deal with openly share. It is highly likely that they are speaking about parts of their life that are important to them and showing respect and interest in those areas builds rapport. This activity should not be conducted with anything other than a desire to connect for the benefit of mutual interest. Your aim is to secure a position and theirs to employ a potential value-adding candidate. Value can be added in many ways and your most positive attributes might be intangible without continued interaction. This is particularly true if you have humorous nature. Judicious use of this cements rapport and shows a lighter element of your character which could be particularly important for a client facing role.

Taking advice

Throughout the networking process you will encounter characters from a broad spectrum of backgrounds, some of which will be very different to your own. As is human nature, each will offer advice with varying levels of value. All advice will add value to your experience even if it at times it appears irrelevant, or at worst patronising. Consider, for example, that you are hoping to become an expert in valuing residential property. If you are not trained, an alternative method may be to view many properties, attend auctions and interact with estate agents. In this instance you attempt to understand the property market through internal and informal research. As part of this you seek to understand the drivers that cause purchasers in your area to commit to a deal. Could it be a high-quality school catchment area? A picturesque view? Or proximity to a major train station? Developing your network can follow a similar pattern. By interacting with individuals from a variety of sectors and backgrounds you will identify patterns and techniques. Part of this process will involve receiving advice from these varied sources and selecting the best elements to keep. Note that your value proposition at each meeting will also be different. Some may be recruiters actively seeking new candidates for their own network or business. Many will simply be willing to help a member of the military. The advice you receive should be framed with the context in which it was delivered.

Should you spot a common trend in your interactions, consider why this might be the case. For example, if you feel that you are regularly patronised or that you are treated in a dismissive manner, assess your own actions. Do you conduct yourself in a way that might encourage such behaviour from others? Equally, if your interactions are mostly positive, consider ways in which you can further refine your approach to achieve results. If those you connect with see you as personable, smart and intelligent, perhaps you need to take more risk in industries that offer a more lucrative (but equally a more challenging) package? In either case a complacent approach on your part is unlikely to support a positive end result for your career search.

Keep a diary of your experiences during networking events and meetings. This will help you to recall key details and assist should you have to offer advice to a friend or colleague. It should be noted that once your own transition is complete it is likely that others will come to you for advice on developing their own employment plans. While this may appear somewhat removed from your current situation it will happen unexpectedly. The lessons you learn at this stage will be invaluable to those seeking to forge their own path and there is much to be gained from helping others to achieve their goals.

The social side of your network

When actively pursuing contacts in the months prior to my departure from the Royal Navy, there were some who logically questioned whether the time I was spending building contacts was wise. It is true that I could have dedicated this same period to formal applications or concentrated study. I found this to be a personal balance based on your ambitions and personal flexibility. My personal circumstances at the time allowed for extensive travel and I was willing to use leave for this activity above all else. This included the provision of a small travel budget and a re-alignment of my social and personal activities to make way for my networking plans.

My strategy was focussed on long-term relationship building set against the short-term risk of failure. My aim from the outset was self-employment and as such I focussed on building networks of linkable and complementary organisations and individuals. This was at the expense of internships or networking events focussed purely on recruitment for other businesses. There is not optimum timeframe for this activity and having too long to consider your options may lead to inefficiency. It is for this reason that understanding your goals in detail is of such importance early in the process. Your entire networking effort can be optimised around this purpose rather than seeking to try different approaches for different potential outcomes.

Networking need not be consigned to the start of your career transition plan. It is an activity which will continue and will help you to develop opportunities in entirely new areas. Winning business for your new employer, seeking informal advice, sales opportunities or project collaboration are just some areas where your network will assist. I my case my network allowed me to select the business model that was optimised for my future plans and this extended far beyond economic benefits. My living arrangements, friendships and even hobbies have since been positively influenced by the networking activity I conducted years previously.

Sharing information

As your network grows and your ideas develop patterns will form which present opportunities for collaboration between your contacts. At this stage you may not have introduced them and they may even be competitors. This presents you with a dilemma that must be carefully managed.

You may be tempted to demonstrate the strength of your connections by commenting openly on who you know and how you came into contact. I would advise against this. Not only will this expose you to the risk of divulging valuable information regarding your plans, it suggests that you may be indiscrete. To a potential employer or client this is not a positive attribute. Consider the following example.

You are in contact with the Sales Director of Company A, who has suggested that there may be a role for you in the future at her firm. They business sells industrial equipment in markets that you have a good understanding of. You then attend dinner with a senior manager from Company B having met at a military transition networking event. Their business is a competitor of Company A and you learn that Company B export most of their products but want to start selling more domestically. Their initial analysis suggests that they could expand production of mechanical components using existing facilities without a significant increase in production costs. There is an awkward silence once they finish explaining the situation. Do you:

A. Tell them that you are in contact with a senior executive from a competitor and that you would be happy to make an introduction if it was of benefit.

B. Tell them that you don't know much about the UK market but that you know that Company A sells similar equipment at a certain price.

C. Comment broadly that it sounds sensible if production costs are staying the same but new sales opportunities are presenting themselves.

D. Change the subject.

The response you select will depend on your motivations, your integrity and your confidence. Response A may cause your dinner partner to refrain from revealing more information knowing that you are in contact with a competitor.

Response B reveals a trade secret and would suggest gross indiscretion. Pricing information is highly sensitive and not for wider discussion if given to you in confidence. It is very unlikely that a sophisticated commercial operator would revel this information in the first instance.

Response C is sensible but only if it can be expanded upon. Expect your guest to further develop the subject. You may be questioned in detail as to your knowledge base both as a potential employer and in order to seek useful market information that you may possess.

Response D retains the option to withdraw from the subject gracefully. Always keep this option in mind should you venture into topic of conversation where you suspect a conflict of interest may arise.

If you are likely to receive sensitive data about a person or company then expect to be presented with a Non-Disclosure Agreement (NDA) to sign. Presented before any valuable information is shared, this is a legal document and breaching it can have serious consequences. If presented with an NDA be sure to read it and do not hesitate to take it away and show a solicitor prior to signature. Scrutinise all elements of such a document. Ensure you understand fully the terms to which you will be held. An NDA can be "one way" (protecting one party from information sharing by another) or "mutual" (protecting both from each other) and there will typically be a time limit placed on the agreement. Also note that in the event that you are starting a business with and wish to protect your own position, an NDA can be used to protect your trade secrets or plans when discussing them with a new party.

Signing contracts

Occasionally a potential employer or client may ask you sign a contract very early in your relationship. While this is rare it can have such significant implications that it is worth of note.

A party will most likely ask you to commit to work for or with them because they have identified that you will create more wealth for them than you cost. Resist the temptation to quickly accept and consider the wider context of such an offer. Can you deliver the outputs that the other party will demand? What are the personal and professional risks? What is the contract missing which might expose you to unforeseen risk?

If working in an area of deep specialist knowledge there may be a contractual clause limiting your ability to work in the same area in the future. Is this tolerable should the contract ruminate prematurely? Imagine a pilot signing a contract with a low-cost airline that prevents her from working for any other operator for two years after contract signature. The pilot signs the document, but six months later, the airline goes out of business and she is made redundant. According to the original agreement, she cannot use her main skill to earn a fair salary for another eighteen months, regardless of the circumstance.

This example is purposely extreme to illustrate a subtle point. There is no need to rush when reading a contract. If you don't understand the contents, query them or ask for more time to consider the terms. Do not be afraid to ask for changes, provided they are reasonable in the business context. Whatever the situation, do not sign any documents without reading them in detail.

Making notes

A development from contractual considerations are the wider implications of putting your intentions in writing. Whether a text message, social media contribution, an e-mail or hand written letter, material you create is admissible to you. If you enter a dispute with an employer or client all of your correspondence and any public content can be scrutinised. If relevant it can provide useful information to competitors and allies alike. As such, think about what you publicise and be prepared for it to be examined forensically by any person or organisation wishing to gain an insight into your capabilities.

In the military I would think nothing of responding to e-mails quickly. While this implies efficiency it can also add risk to your correspondence. Consider how a piece of seemingly innocuous writing could be interpreted should circumstances change. In the commercial environment this is of vital importance, as a sharp supplier or customer could attempt to negotiate around informal commitments made in ill-considered correspondence. Remember that once sent you have lost control of your material. In the majority of cases this will be of little consequence, but in some significant instances it could cause significant harm to your reputation.

A network of networks

Growing and developing your contacts can be a thoroughly rewarding process. As your confidence grows you will become a connector of others and a catalyst for new activity. This not only cements your reputation but offers new opportunities for both your business and social activities. A close friend of mine often points out that if you do something you love you never work a day in your life. In my experience this is true and building a network is a vital part of the journey to such deep personal fulfilment.

8 BASIC BUSINESS STRUCTURES

We will examine large and small organisational structures, a comparison to the military and some considerations when approaching either organisation. Remember, every business you interact with will have norms and values which may be somewhat different to those marketed publicly. Keep an open mind to allow for these new discoveries, particularly once you become more acquainted with a particular organisation.

You may not have considered the differences between large and small companies before. Consider the differences you have experienced between large military formations and small specialised groups. One has resilience (spare resources), significant capability across a wide range of areas and an ability to take on many projects at the same time. The smaller unit is targeted in its efforts but has far less capacity. It is likely to have a much deeper level of expert knowledge but in a narrow field. While these rules do not describe perfectly every organisation (military or otherwise) they are good metrics from which to start.

Large firms

For the purposes of this book large companies are those comparable in size or larger to one of the UK Armed Forces, or a major formation within an armed force. Staff numbers will be in the thousands and the associated corporate structure will be hierarchical. The business is likely to have a significant national and international presence. The products and services offered to the market may be applicable to a number of separate sectors and customers (oil and gas, management consultancy, financial services). A well-established selection and recruitment process for employees is likely to exist, provided by both third party agencies and internally.

What follows is a diagram outlining the basic structure of such a business. This diagram aims to give you the broadest possible overview of how a large business might be structured and I recommend that you use it as a start point for more detailed research in your chosen industry.

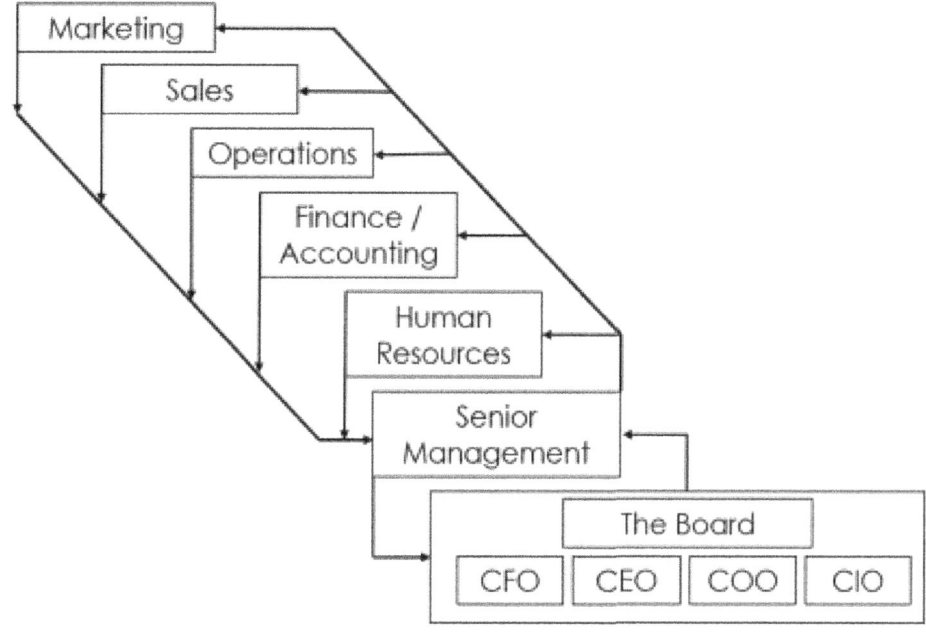

In this example each part of the business aims to feed a sales process which offers products and services in exchange for money, "revenue". The structure above could apply to many businesses, from a ceramics manufacturer to an independent financial advisory group. The specifics of each department vary by business activity but this diagram is a good starting point for anyone looking to understand basic business processes.

Each part of the organisation has specific objectives, set by the management team (labelled here as "The Board") and fed down in a manner that will be familiar to anyone who has operated in a military structure. In business, interactions may be far less formal than you have experienced before, but the principles of a hierarchy remain comparable to those of the Armed Forces. There are likely to be layers of approval and authority for any decision making, teams are likely to be large and the terms and conditions of employment will be well established. Such employment terms may be open to limited alteration and negotiation (albeit more than those in the military are). Each business unit is set specific goals to reach on behalf of shareholders. The shareholder, or owners of the business, expect adherence to a defined corporate strategy that aims to maximise profit. Increasingly this strategy is expected to conform to stringent corporate social responsibility guidelines.

The term corporate social responsibility refers to those activities which are conducted in a way sympathetic to both society and the environment rather than simply to maximise profit. Globally, investors are increasingly conscious of social and environmental issues that in the past were either ignored, overlooked, or simply beyond the comprehension of society at the time. A large firm is likely to have a corporate social responsibility policy, and it is worth researching this if available prior to any interview.

Certain industries will have nuanced business units, or divisions. For example, an investment bank may have an investment banking division, and equities division, a compliance division, operations division, human resources and risk. A steelmaker, however, will be more focussed on physical supply chain management of raw materials, health and safety, onward logistics of finished product and sales. As such the business will evolve with business units that reflect this alternative focus. The aim of both organisations, however, is to generate profit. The investment bank may do so by brokering large company mergers, selling stocks on the stock exchange on behalf of businesses at a premium, or engaging in significant foreign exchange currency transactions. The steelmaker tries to sell finished steel to customers such as car manufacturers for the highest price it can, while keeping the cost of production as low as possible (minimal labour, stable raw material suppliers, efficient energy consumption in smelting). Both types of business are aiming to sell something in a way more compelling than their competitors, but their vastly different products reflect their different resultant structures.

Large companies like this will appeal to those who seek stability after a potentially unpredictable or dynamic military career. There will often be greater choice of location and promotion while the salary may be comparable to a military equivalent. These firms also offer a strong foundation from which to build commercial knowledge and are often a prestigious name to add to your CV. I still believe that the first role you commit to after military service defines you disproportionately in employment terms for some time. This is because you remain an unknown quantity for civilian employers until you have shown your capabilities in the market. In this context working for a well-known and respected firm is a sound choice.

Unless you have a connection in a relevant part of the company you applying for, your CV will have to navigate a significant human resources (HR) system. This process is likely to be stringent and unforgiving and may discount your CV if key words or qualifications are absent. For example, many banks and major consultancies stipulate a degree as an entry requirement (often regardless of subject) and if you don't have one you may not get through the "HR filter". This is where military insight days offer a significant advantage. They provide an avenue for your CV out-with the normal process and offer you a higher likelihood of future recruitment. If you can secure and interview and sell your capabilities, the detail of your CV may become a secondary consideration. The similarities between large businesses and military structures also mean that should the institutional aspects of service life frustrate you, a large business may not offer the optimum alternative.

Such a firm might offer greater stability, predictable progression and sound benefits but the constraints imposed on your time may be comparable to the career you are leaving. While the military can offer extreme examples of working conditions or time spent away from family, the same can sometimes be said of large businesses. While the physical conditions are likely to be less volatile, hours physically in the workplace and spent on your commute may be more demanding.

When considering these factors I experienced a change in my ambitions from large corporate body to self-employment. I noted that my adult working life had been spent entirely in an institutional military setting. While I am proud of my time in service and found it immensely enjoyable, I concluded that a change was needed. The widely held wisdom among my cohort was that a large institution would be the optimum course of action and I found that military transition programmes are well placed to assist with this path.

Small firms

For the purposes of this section small firms are simply those which exhibit characteristics similar to those shown by specialist military units. The definition of a "small" business will vary from one sector to another. For example, there are cases where businesses that employ very few people are worth millions of pounds due to their distinct product or service. It is too simplistic to characterise businesses by employee numbers but a useful comparison can be made by considering how quickly you might progress in such an organisation, compared to a larger equivalent.

Small firms could be run by small groups of entrepreneurs, families, or one person. They could be niche tech firms, independent building companies, small restaurant chains or boutique consultancies. They have some competitive advantages over their larger counterparts. For example, they can often react quickly to complex market changes with minimal time spent seeking approval for their plans or considering strategies. In theory, by being small their revenue will be lower than that of a large company in the same industry and so they will be forced to be more efficient. That is of course a theoretical suggestion. For our purpose I will focus on how the physical size of these businesses affects your approach, rather than their pure profitability.

My own experience of small and medium sized businesses stems from growing up in a family that ran such a company and now starting my own. The diagram that follows reflects both my own experiences and information gleaned from interviews and research.

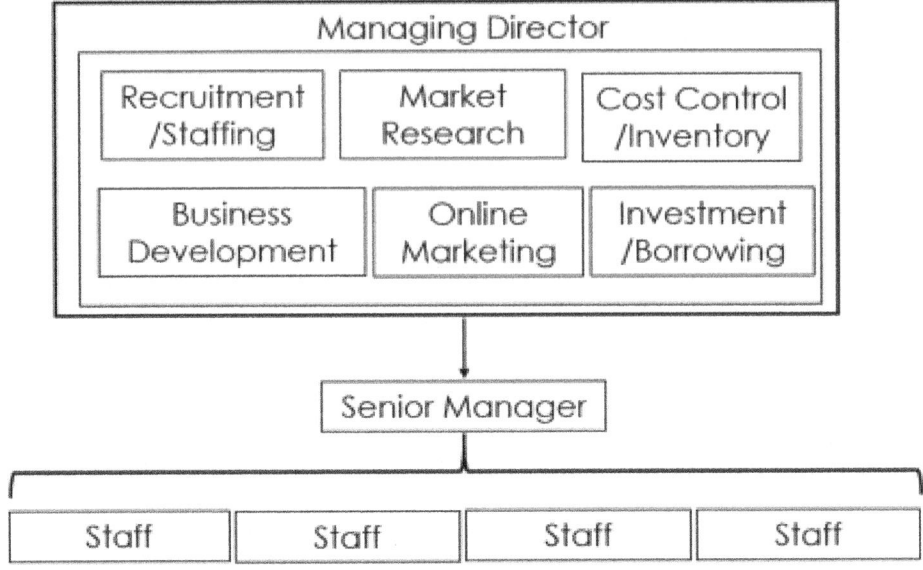

The diagram shown is somewhat different from that which I used to describe a large firm. Here the Managing Director may or may not be the business owner. They will be the leader of a number of Directors each of whom have responsibility for a specific function. Alternatively, a small number of Directors may be responsible for more than one area each. They will either be employed by the owner to run the business or will coincidentally also be the main shareholder in the business. In the example I have used the Managing Director (or simply Director if there is no single designated MD) takes many of the decisions that in a larger business are shared by a board and shaped by a team of senior managers. In a small firm the Managing Director may be able to ask one or two trusted senior advisers for guidance and advice. They may also use these individuals to keep a close eye on the day to day workings of the business, from staff behaviour to customer complaints.

With such small size come some disadvantages. Unlike a large company, a small business may not have the legal or commercial power to take major competitive risks in their market. By the same token, their ability to "carry" underperforming staff will be reduced meaning that you will have to add value straight away and may have more responsibility early on. This can have benefits to you as an employee. Like the military, large companies whose headquarters may be in a different region or country operate with hierarchies that sometimes make access to senior management difficult. You may not achieve such exposure to senior leaders until well established in the organisation. In small firms, should you prove to be effective, opportunities to interact with senior members of the business may come sooner. This can lead to rapid promotion within your new organisation.

Smaller businesses are likely to offer less flexibility in terms of working location, but this is increasingly offset by many firms encouraging working from home. In my experience, small firms can be exciting and rewarding organisations to work for or with and I would strongly encourage you to interview with some.

Whereas large companies may have distinct business units dedicated to one business area, in smaller firms you can find one person or office covering many functions. This relates to efficiency and scale. A marketing officer for a business supplying lawn- mowers to maintenance contractors is likely to also support sales activity and budgeting for the next year. When I started my business, I was covering marketing, sales, recruitment, project management, management accounting and due diligence. Joining an experienced business partner helped the firm to mature but our workload did not reduce. By navigating this process I learned the mechanics of business, in particular those elements which influence others most acutely.

Self-employment

Have you ever considered working for yourself? The modern-day image of a technology start-up often conjures images of relaxed working conditions, casual dress, shared office space and a sense of relaxed creativity. Although my business does in parts fall into the "tech start-up" category, my experience is far from this idyllic vision.

Although the reality of self-employment is somewhat more challenging than many imagine it has given me a sense of purpose and excitement not felt since I first joined the Naval Service. There are many risks and a coherent strategy must be refined while also retaining the flexibility needed to meet new opportunities. The early stages of such a venture see founding shareholders carrying out a myriad of roles to maximise efficiency and retain an element of agility. Helpfully such a process is a concentrated and effective way to develop your business acumen, negotiating skills and resilience while creating your own products and services.

You will learn quickly how and when to bring in external assistance while also becoming accustomed to decision making in a new environment. The crux of your entire business will be financial solvency and an ability to survive unexpected setbacks. This will test your appetite for risk long-held perceptions regarding your character to new limits. The process also exposes your integrity in ways that may be new to you. Consider the following example. A client asks you to put together a sales forecast for a product that you have helped them source to support marketing strategy. After interviews and some joint analysis, you quote for five days of work at a fixed daily rate of pay. The client is content and signs the contract for the work to be carried out.

After three days of work you realise that you have misquoted and that you can deliver the work in four days comfortably, potentially saving the client a full day of payment (or in this case 20% of their costs for using your services). What do you do?

There is a clear distinction between an honest mistake, building in extra time on a high-risk project and misleading the client. There are certainly situations where one might incorporate extra time to test or refine a product or service prior to delivery. This is good practice and protects the client in the long run. If, however, you have made a mistake through naivete, an appropriate course of action would be to pass the saving back to the client. This bring numerous potential positive outcomes. Although you will lose 20% of your quoted fee, you also free up time to search for or do other work without risk of breaching your contract (which may stipulate that during client time you are prohibited from doing work for other projects, or conducting business development activity). There are also longer-term commercial benefits that outweigh your lower fee. The client is likely to respect your honesty and efficiency. Provided the work is to the standard expected this assist in winning repeat business and a positive referral to others.

I have focussed on self-employment in the field of professional services, more commonly known as management consultancy. Many other types of activity can be commercialised and you may find a model that suits you particularly well. Some of the best advice I have received was from a retired commercial lawyer; "your strategy is about what you don't do. Don't take on work just because you think you need it". These words have stayed with me and I have tried to apply this mantra to my activity. It has required self-discipline, a healthy risk appetite and a willingness to endure. Taking scheduled "days off" is not part of my model, but for others a conventional five day schedule works well. That is not to suggest that inefficient working is to be encouraged. It is merely to highlight that when there is work to be done, it is done as soon as possible regardless of the date or time.

Start-up finance is a tricky subject for those not accustomed to financial instruments. During my final years in the Naval Service I would commute on the tube. I noticed during my tenure that advertisements for start-up loans and new types of finance were pervasive, targeting East-London based technology firms with easy access capital. These loans and crowdfunding options have many advantages, particularly if you already have confirmed demand for a product or service. They are not a sound option if you have not yet formed a coherent business plan. The decision to either sell equity in your business or borrow from a third party should be considered very carefully.

I made extensive use of self-education tools during the early stages of business setup. I continue to find open source material very useful in guiding my research prior to delving deeper into a particular area. Resources I commonly made use of included online videos, subject specific books, advice from my network and business short courses. Should you embark on a similar path do not underestimate the time commitment that such learning entails. In the effort to refine my choice on which products and services to create and market I found two books particularly useful. The first is entitled *"Competing Against Luck"* and is written by Harvard Business School Professor Clayton M Christensen.[21] He and three other leading business academics discuss "Jobs Theory". They suggest that when we buy products and services as consumers, we do so to solve a problem in our lives. In other words we employ the product to do a job in the same way a business employs a person to fulfil a demand. As such, in order to decide whether something to be sold will be successful, an entrepreneur should first consider what problem the product is solving and how suitable it is compared to other options for solving the same problem.

Take the following example. On weekday mornings a salesman goes to a coffee shop near his home to grab a quick take-away coffee for his business partner. He could of course make his own coffee and put it in a flask. Why go to the coffee shop? What problem does the coffee shop solve that his home-made attempts do not solve as effectively?

Firstly, the coffee shop makes better coffee than he does. This is not important to him, but he would rather give his business partner a high-quality coffee as their first interaction of the day. This gets them off to a good start and shows among other things mutual respect and a willingness to go to extra lengths. Secondly, by buying take-away coffees they something to drink while they talk in the car on the way to their office. As such the coffee needs to be hot enough to last the whole journey and neither of them can make coffee that hot that quickly at home. Thirdly, if they make a coffee at home hot enough to last the journey, they probably do not have time to properly clean their coffee makers before going to work.

This is an abstract example, but the coffee shop makes profit from these customers because it solves three problems. Number one, it sets the tone for a good day in partnership that might otherwise pass un-noticed. Number two, it makes coffee that stays hot for the entire car journey because it uses a proper espresso machine and steamer. Number three, the customers do not have to clean their own coffee making apparatus as soon as they get home from a long day at work.

Search for tasks around you that are difficult or imperfect and imagine how you might alleviate those issues. Do you see something where a new product or service could make a difference? Jobs theory may help you create a business idea from seemingly everyday situations and in my experience is very powerful when considering what to do next with one's business plans.

The second book, "What they don't teach you at Harvard" by Mark McCormack[22], focuses on the behaviours of successful business people. The late author pioneered sports sponsorship in the United States, eventually becoming responsible for global sporting events and their participants (such as Wimbledon tennis). His book, now decades old, still provides an excellent handrail to the practical realities of organising and completing deals, business correspondence and explaining the rationale of successful commercial operators. There has since been a follow-on title[23] where associates of McCormack describe in their own words his leadership style. His ability to value his employees and associates encouraged them to work to their best.

An Alternative Perspective

Louise Lane is an experienced Accountant and commercial property portfolio manager with over thirty years of experience in retail, property management and development. For much of that time she acted as a board-level adviser to a multi-million-pound family enterprise.

How do small businesses really work? How do individuals bring their ideas to reality? It is a balance of freedom versus security.

When I was approached to contribute to this book I was asked to offer an unbiased answer to the questions posed above. It is not a straightforward response as each business is an individual entity with it's own characteristics and challenges. An examination of how a small business is formed, from concept to reality, will hopefully offer insights into how such an enterprise functions. A business is only ever as good as it's management team and for a small business in infancy, that might just be you!

The safety net of being employed in the public sector, with a guaranteed monthly salary, paid holiday entitlement, accruing pension rights and support does not exist in the entrepreneurial community. This may be compounded by the fact well-meaning individuals might questioning your decision and judgement to even consider becoming self-employed and all that it entails. This apparent negativity can be deflected as through your previous military career you will have fortuitously gained many transferable skills that others are unlikely to have.

When discussing transferable skills which could be applied to running a business, large or small, the principles remain the same; reactive and intuitive decision making, foresight, tenacity, self- discipline, planning, adherence to parameters and the ability to meet deadlines. Most importantly of all, a sound grasp of common sense.

There are four themes to keep uppermost in your mind, "Why, How, When, What if ?" Write down each of these and expand upon each prior to embarking on a detailed business plan.

"Why"- What are the reasons that have prompted to you to decide to make the decision to run your own business.

"How"- Will your idea provide a service, product or strategy that improves an existing process. You need to calculate a budget which should include realistic revenue and expenses, together with an additional contingency fund of six months estimated expenses. Speak to accountants and lawyers who offer an initial free discussion to gain an insight into the mechanics of setting up a business. Based on your initial interactions select those professionals who made the process of setting up a business clear and understandable. Also consider how transparent they are regarding the fees that they charge for undertaking any further work. Many parts of the running of the business, such as keeping financial records, may be best served by third parties (such as book-keepers). Keeping records yourself in the early stages allows you to have tighter cost control and to understand when you are likely to break even on specific projects.

This is where selecting the right accountant is important. They can help you prepare a realistic budget, offer advice on the financial records that need to be kept and guide you through any tricky financial forms relating to the business. Using a simple accounts software package can provide a basic daily snapshot of the business, which is vital. Not only will this feature help you control your overheads it could reduce the cost of your accountancy fee when your accountant prepares and submits your annual accounts. If your business expands you may decide to employ staff and your accountant can process the payroll for the business.

Engaging a solicitor who is able to explain as simply as possible the legal position of the business is essential. The principles for the selection of a legal advisor are similar to those of selecting an accountant. Ensure that you fully understand the fee structure of the service provider and that you can form an effective working relationship.

"When" - Although it is possible to set up a business quickly this is rarely the best way to proceed. Take time to plan your desired evolution of the business. It is sometimes possible piggy-back on the product or concept of the moment for short-term gain but this is unlikely to be a sustainable strategy. "Time in" the market is more valuable than simply "timing" the market.

"What if?" - Give your business a chance to establish with a realistic timeline based on how much you are willing to commit in resources to support it. Have definite points at which you will walk away from the business if certain conditions are not met. Many successful entrepreneurs have suffered many setbacks on the route to attaining their goals. Tenacity, combined with a willingness to walk away from an idea at the right moment, will have carried them through these difficult times. There are significant advantages to establishing a small but well-run operation and remaining as such. A small but well-run enterprise can exercise tight cost control and can react swiftly to market changes. The ability to survive the unexpected is just as important as growth, as illustrated by recent global events.

While there are significant benefits to the security of being employed I feel that the sense of freedom that comes with running a business of your own. Your military career will have equipped you with a strong foundation and the potential to develop sound business acumen.

Whatever you decide to do next, good luck!

Your next steps

I hope your reading has given you not only alternative perspectives but also a deeper understanding of your ambitions and capabilities. This book may in fact motivate you to remain in the military or your current career while you consolidate your thinking and refine your plan.

If indeed these perspectives cause you to remain in place, even for just a short while, then consider this a success. In my experience, a decision to leave an organisation which has as much influence over your life as the Armed Forces should not be taken lightly. Similarly, changing course having established a routine can be difficult. Despite these considerations the requirement to change can be in reaction to an unexpected and overwhelming stimulus. Reactive situations are by their nature difficult to predict and take require personal investment to mitigate without taking significant risk. As such, this book may assist you in pacing your decision making in order to mitigate the unexpected. My final year of service was a constant evolution of ideas, courses of action and eventually actionable decisions with tangible consequences. Visualising this change is an abstract challenge when serving at sea, in the field or in even at home.

Reflect on your learning so far, augmented by ideas that this book has given you. Perhaps that will lead to a self-employment business plan, a course to prepare you for a job interview, or a decision to take time with your family on completion of your service. Your personal risk appetite combined with your ambition will assist you in selecting the optimum course of action.

Be prepared for situation where you fail in your first attempts. This failure could be minor, or feel catastrophic, but try to view it in the context of your longer-term transition. It is important to welcome failure as a method of learning, but to do so in a manageable and positive manner. For example, if starting a business, selecting an area where you possess familiarity or passion will reduce risk and allow you to manoeuvre more effectively around setbacks. This is linked to your financial resilience and the level of earning at which you are comfortable.

Similarly, interview applications may be fraught with disappointing interviews and at times patronising advice. I met quite a number of individuals during my transition who claimed to have applied for significant numbers of roles with no success. My thoughts on hearing these examples of challenge and failure are mixed. Based on basic analysis, at some point (possibly after five rejections) those individuals might be better placed by completely re-evaluating their approach. Whether the locations of the roles to the way their CV was written, repeated rejection is a sign that those elements that can be changed should be re-examined and modified. There are clearly other factors beyond the control of the job seeker. Wider economic growth, political stability and global trends all affect recruitment at both local and national levels. If experiencing repeated rejection, consider abstract or alternative roles. Remain at all times willing to compromise and learn whatever is required. A dogmatic approach will likely lead to disappointment in all but the rarest cases.

My personal example is a little unconventional but the path I followed mirrors many of the experiences you may encounter. I investigated salaried employment options and met impressive people from a wide range of organisations. I opted for self-employment and ultimately business partnership because I saw an opportunity to fulfil my core motivations for work. The research, networking and preparation conducted prior to establishing my business is not wasted but instead applied differently to my current situation.

Having a conversation about your next steps with loved ones and friends allows those of greatest importance to understand why you are choosing a particular path. This is very important if you are entering a completely new sector or having to move and change long-term family plans. Each situation brings with it different relationships to manage. I recommend keeping those you care about appraised of your courses of action as plans develop. It would be an unfortunate outcome to succeed in military transition but lose the relationships that are dearest to you in the process. Close family and friends can offer helpful alternative perspectives. This is helpful if your single-minded focus prevents you from seeing otherwise obvious pitfalls in your plans.

There are many organisations willing to offer help to service leavers, both with business plans and corporate employment opportunities. Use as many as you deem necessary to achieve your goals. There is no format for the level of engagement you should commit to or how to successfully divide your time. In terms of networking, these groups offer an invaluable source of ideas and connections. I recommend that you make the most of these and attend events as regularly as your schedule allows. You may even go back to some once you have successfully transitioned and offer to support other service leavers.

The system which allows us to leave roles in the Armed Forces and be presented with opportunities relies on the diligence, kindness and time given up by enterprising and loyal people in a wide range of sectors. Not all are former servicepeople, but all are keen to help you succeed. Such a system functions best if it is regenerated with new volunteers and new ideas. I recommend that once your own future stabilises, you give up a little of your time to help others. The rewards of doing so far outweigh investment in time and energy required.

9 NOVEL IDEAS FOR JOB SEEKERS

There are many tried and tested methods for finding work. In this chapter I hope to give you some thoughts on personal administration during this process which can be applied across sectors or large organisations. The same techniques can be modified for finding clients for a new business, particularly when supported by a systematic marketing plan.

Personalised business cards

I am an advocate of the personal business card. As a new jobseeker this demonstrates initiative and an awareness of your personal marketing effort. It also shows understanding of the basics of networking in a commercial setting.

There is a limit to the cost and time you should invest in producing this product, and to the design and type of card selected. I have noticed the increasing trend to have metallic or patterned cards. While this may make a striking first impression, be cautious with how you use them. They are much more expensive to produce and could give an impression of expense and high fees on your part. While this might be of benefit once you are established commercially, in the early stages there will be little known about your personal value and capabilities. A plain product printed professionally on high-grade card is sufficient.

I avoid elaborate text on my cards. Your personal impression should be the lasting memory, not the complexity of your business card. A particularly memorable business card will stand out in a pile of other cards but may detract from a core attribute that you were hoping to convey in your first meeting. I recently received a business card where the individual had printed their face on it. I am personally not an advocate of this approach but if you choose to incorporate this into your design, ensure the photograph is professionally taken. It should reflect the level of quality you hope to add to the organisation receiving it.

Writing letters

This is a labour intensive but potentially powerful way in which to leave an impression or reach a specific person in an organisation. A personal letter on high-grade writing paper and written with a good ink-cartridge pen has more impact than almost any other non-verbal form of communication. Producing such work takes time and may require several drafts due to mistakes or imperfect layout. As such use this method sparingly but do include it in your communications plan. It is simply good manners to follow up on any one to one or specific group meeting with a letter to thank the host and offer further correspondence if appropriate.

If writing a letter, make sure that the layout follows business convention. There are many online resources demonstrating this and a proper layout sets the tone for your values and standards. Note that all aspects of your behaviour and correspondence form professional and personal impression. Small victories such as well written letters and professional business cards add significant value to your overall offering.

Job seeking on the move

In the latter stages of your time service will have access to significant amounts of leave. Alternatively, you may be seeking work having left the Armed Forces. For many this period is one of intensive job-seeking and this may require significant amounts of travel. Such a task requires thorough planning if you are to present yourself professionally at each interaction.

There are some basic rules to follow which will assist:

- *For a week of travel, I recommend two suits and a clean shirt for every day.*
- *Stay at locations which offer the facility to iron your clothing and have access to free Wifi.*
- *Keep a detailed diary of any meetings and connections, updating it at the end of each day and any meal-breaks.*
- *If hiring a car, ensure it is as economical as possible, but also comfortable.*

Plan your travel around clusters of potential employers or clients. If you can meet with three or four firms in a region then do so with a clear strategy and strict timelines.

Protecting data

In pursuit of potential employers or clients you may amass significant amount of contact data. Be wary of regulations regarding data storage and use. This is particularly pertinent if you elect to publicise your activity on social media or business networking sites. If you intend to start a business consider attending a basic cyber-security course or aligning yourself with government standards on the basics of data security. There are numerous online guides which can help you and accreditations which demonstrate a basic level of cyber-security in your business and personal IT. Such accreditations are inexpensive and offer another opportunity to both demonstrate initiative and sensitivity to a pertinent issue.

Corporate hosting

When engaging with new contacts and organisations limit your alcohol intake so as not to compromise your train of thought or decision making. There is a temptation when being hosted by a corporate body to over-indulge. This can lead to a variety of difficult situations, from social awkwardness to poor decisions. My grandfather would occasionally describe his first interview after his last sea-going role. He had applied for a position in a merchant bank (a term which describes what we would now call an investment or corporate lender). He was considering a new career in maritime insurance and had replied to an advert in a national paper. The selection process looked straightforward and all of the applicants were treated to an elaborate lunch in Liverpool, with wine and beer. Then, a few drinks in, they were given a surprise actuarial maths and English literature test.

Thankfully he got the job. It is rare for this kind of selection to happen now (it is probably illegal!) but your behaviour under the influence of alcohol and your willingness to accept "free" drinks from a corporate host leaves an impression. Tread with caution if presented with this scenario.

Language claims

If you are confident in the use of a language other than English, consider including this in your job seeking. Learning another language is an impressive trait. Be cautious of over-promising in an area where you have little recent practice. Sophisticated employers may elect to include a first-language speaker in your selection process to test any claims. Be prepared for this eventuality and use it to your advantage where possible. A seamless transition from English to an alternative is very impressive but requires a significant level of competence and confidence.

Offering to work for free

I have been counselled by some service leavers that offering to work for nothing creates a positive lasting impression and provides access to an organisation that might otherwise not be possible. Despite this, I advise that you avoid a situation where you are expected to work without an agreed level of remuneration.

When considering my business plan I investigated offering free consultancy in the early stages to prove myself to clients who hadn't worked with me before. I quickly decided against this after further research. Businesspeople understand that you need to charge if offering a service and working for free suggests either desperation or naivety. You may still elect to negotiate around a reduced fee up on an initial project or a reduced salary during a "probation" period with a new employer. In this instance it is important to establish clear conditions on when this period will end and what the associated package will revert to. This will allow you to make informed financial plans whilst also avoiding unexpected and awkward negotiations for your employer or client. If you can't reach a mutually agreeable position, seeking other opportunities may be a more appropriate course of action. While there are examples of individuals offering to carry out work for free and subsequently being offered a position, commercial wisdom would suggest that this is a suboptimal approach.

Creating a personal website

A personal website performs a similar role to a personalised business card. Producing one is straightforward with a myriad of free online resources explaining the process for those who do not have a computing background. My first site was produced over two weeks and cost a small monthly fee to maintain and improve. A professional business site, with members areas and payment vehicles is best produced by a professional agency. If your site will simply display information and contact details a self-built option can yield professional and effective results.

The site should appear unambiguous and offer a clear route to contacting you. If the main purpose is to provide a personal overview for the purpose of job-seeking, consider an up to date and refined networking site profile before producing a web page. Dedicated networking profiles cost less to maintain and scoured by recruiters on a regular basis. By comparison, unless investment is allocated to search engine optimisation, a personal site will not feature highly in an internet search.

Enjoy the process

Searching for future employment opportunities can be debilitating but it should also be viewed in the context of positive change. The process will introduce you to new people from industries and backgrounds that are likely to be completely new. This will afford you ample opportunities for self-development both inside and outside the commercial environment. Approaching your transition with a positive, focussed mentality will engender trust in those you meet and a willingness to engage with you beyond first impression. Keep your humility, your sense of humour and your ambition close to hand and positive outcomes will follow.

10 THE ECONOMY AND INDUSTRIES

In this chapter I will outline some major industrial sectors that trade in the UK and include relevant parallels and differences to a military system. These are my findings based on research and interactions. In using this chapter for further research consider at all times two distinct distinctions. The first is the distinct character of public sector working when compared to the private sector. This particular distinction characterises not just the military, but the civil service, NHS and other centrally funded public bodies. The second is the unique character of military service when compared to all other roles, regardless of whether in the public or private sector.

The structure of the UK economy is similar in nature to the economies of other Western capitalist powers. The academic and economic terms used to describe this structure in detail are ones that you may be familiar with. They are often used in the media and regular reading of the business section of a quality newspaper will help you become more comfortable with their meaning.

The traditional model of a capitalist economy comprises three industrial groups; primary, secondary and tertiary.[24] Primary industry concerns the extraction of raw materials, such as quarrying and mining of ores for further uses (for example, iron ore for use in steel production). Secondary industries concern the manufacturing of products using processed raw materials. In the mentioned example, a car factory making use of finished steel would constitute secondary industry. Tertiary industry concerns services which do not directly involve raw material extraction or manufacturing of products. For example, a car wash, a management consultancy or a retail outlet all sit in the tertiary sector, commonly known as the "service" sector.

The industrial revolution, which was initiated in Britain but soon spread across other Western nations completely changed the way that jobs were created and supported. The economy we live in today owes its foundations to this industrial change. The advent of the steam engine, new smelting methods for metals and subsequent improved infrastructure allowed land-owners and investors to create mechanised factories. This mechanisation allowed them to produce products on a large scale (refined into a process known as "mass production"). These processes required large amounts of labour in order to operate and so migration to cities, where these factories were located, occurred. The reliance on water to both turn water-wheels and be heated by coal to produce steam meant that many of these factories and foundries were situated near to rivers and coastlines. The same can be said of the need to import and export, which required sailing ships to bring in imported raw materials and export finished products. Examining a map of the UK shows that most of our major cities are found around the coast or on major rivers. Even Birmingham and Manchester, both located inland, are connected to other cities by a vast system of canals and railways.

Prior to the establishment of these industrial centres rural populations farmed in small communities and lived in crofting type settlements. Many of these people then migrated to the new cities to find work in mostly primary and secondary industry. This history is relevant to you because you can draw the effects it has had through to your search for work. During the twentieth century, many other nations began to compete with traditional Western economies in manufacturing and raw material extraction. Their costs were (and are) lower, they have faster population growth to service new industries and sadly their populations are often willing to work in less regulated conditions.

The result has been a pivot for Western economies towards the tertiary or service sector as nations become globally reliant on each other for different parts of the value creation process. For example, China is now the leading global manufacturer (secondary industry), Saudi Arabia is a major crude oil extractor and producer (primary industry) and Britain is a centre of global finance alongside New York and Singapore (tertiary industry).

This process, known as globalisation, is the reason that many of the jobs available in the UK are in the service sector. You may possess qualifications in aerospace or marine engineering meaning you have a niche skill set that gives you access to secondary industry positions, but most advertised roles are in the service sector.[25] The social and political impact of this change is well explained in *Hillbilly Elegy*, a first-hand account of how economic changes globally affect voting patterns and social choices.[26] Although not strictly an academic account the author gives insightful detail of how globalisation affected his previously heavy-industry based community.

The UK is increasingly known for a rapidly growing technology sector which encompasses those businesses focussed on cutting edge research leading to new innovations. These may take the form of mobile phone applications, data analytics tools for business or artificial intelligence software. The sector is focussed around East London but there are impressive examples in many major cities. These start-ups often have a culture that is very different from the military but this can offer a major advantage in their areas of business.

The charities sector is now a major employer in the UK and with the decline in primary and secondary industries, this is now referred to as "third sector" (in more recent times people having started referring to "manufacturing", "services" and the "third sector" when describing Western economies). Your military skills can add enormous value to disadvantaged groups through work in this area. I recommend dedicated research into opportunities with both military and non-military focussed charities if this is an area you had not considered before.

Specific industries

The sectors are sub-divided into industries. Primary sector industries, with their focus on raw material extraction and agriculture, include coal, fishing, livestock and arable farming, and quarrying. Secondary industries include such examples as car manufacturing, production, food processing and industrial equipment production. Tertiary industries are broader still and include road haulage, childcare, banking and casino management. Any role you apply for will sit within a sector and be part of an industry. As such, once a suitable role has been identified, research the following prior to interview:

- *Sector trends in your country and in a major trading partner. For example, is the service sector in the UK growing? What is happening in the United States?*

- *Industry trends in your country and region. Who are the competitors to the firm you are applying for, has your potential firm featured in the news recently and if so why?*

These two questions will give you an appreciation of the macroeconomic conditions affecting your chosen industry and company. Macroeconomics refers to the study of large-scale or general economic factors, such as interest rates or national productivity.[27] These same factors affect the cost of your mortgage, your energy bills and your taxes so I would encourage you to study them. They are useful metrics to broadly understand whether for professional or personal interest reasons.

We will now examine more closely specific industries that are active in the UK economy. If there is a particular area that interests you then I implore you to both conduct research and read literature with a targeted industry focus. Business journals may offer the most refined and technical information but these can be expensive, so conduct your own general research before committing to any subscriptions. Setting yourself learning goals regarding an industry you know little about can prove both fulfilling and highly fruitful at interview.

Manufacturing

I will focus on the broad themes of UK manufacturing as there are numerous opportunities for ex-service personnel. This is a significant economic sector which could be further dissected and I recommend further reading as required.

You may already be aware that UK manufacturing has seen a decline in both share of gross domestic product and employment since the 1960s. This has been linked macroeconomic factors imposed by both globalisation and changing social trends. The 2008 financial crisis saw attempts by the government to rebalance the economy. In practical terms this meant creating a greater mix of service and manufacturing activities in an effort to create an economy more resilient to future shocks. While this overarching goal is to the benefit of manufacturers, significant challenges remain. The use of "just in time" supply exposes certain industries, particularly car manufacturing, to global economic changes. This supply chain model results in components of parts manufactured elsewhere being imported into UK factories for final vehicle assembly. The car manufacturing industry, until recently used as an example of how UK manufacturing can modernise and remain competitive, now faces major economic pressure. Brexit, European and Bank of England interest rates and any change in demand from consumers in China are particularly powerful macroeconomic factors.[28] Many vehicles manufactured in the UK are exported to fast-growing economies where increasing earnings are allowing populations to afford newer and more expensive personal cars on a large scale. Any change to the fortunes of these populations, such as a slowdown in wage growth in China, will change demand for these vehicles. In turn the decisions made by manufacturers will have a direct impact on your ability to secure lucrative roles in their businesses.

I am an advocate of the UK manufacturing sector, particularly having been exposed to it while working directly for the Ministry of Defence. Many innovative and dynamic businesses are conducting activity that not only benefits national security but also provides highly skilled and well-paid jobs. As a military leaver, many opportunities exist, particularly in smaller companies who seek to win government contracts or refine their operational procedures. Numerous major UK manufacturers have military internship and employment schemes. They are active nationally and options are available regardless of your UK location. Service leavers often perform well in major infrastructure projects where liaison between manufacturing reliant supply chains and project delivery agencies is needed.

In order to better understand the recent history of manufacturing and likely future trends there are a numerous useful resources. I recommend reading "The Unsung Guru", a book describing the life of Professor Lord Kumar Bhattacharyya and his successful efforts developing the Warwick Manufacturing Group (WMG).[29] Having trained as an engineer in a resurgent Indian economy, Bhattacharyya moved to the UK in the late 1960s and was surprised to find manufacturing and engineering firms languishing. He noted worrying comparisons between corporate culture and training in the UK when compared to international competitors, who were excelling. He sought to establish a body that could combine the best of academia and management to give manufacturing executives and workers formalised, practical management training. The history of WMG and of Bhattacharyya is fascinating and the book helps the reader to identify the issues faced in manufacturing and how this might affect the types of role available.

Construction

This sector shares similarities with the military as it has a broad range of roles and areas of work to apply to. This varies from sales and management to practical trade-based roles, such as plumbing and joinery. Employment is highly sensitive to economic growth and contraction. Major infrastructure projects or efforts to increase the number of new build houses available to first-time buyers will encourage firms to recruit provided that economic growth potential exists. In order to be successful in any application it is likely that you will have to commit to some training. This sector has a very competitive labour market with large numbers of people seeking to fill places available. There are exceptions to this, with both practical and management roles in specialist areas experiencing a labour shortage. Research will identify which areas these are linked to specific projects.

Projects could be nationwide and an expectation to travel is required, as well as unpredictable working hours (unless you are on a contract involving shift work). Organisational culture is likely to mirror many aspects of the military, particularly when on site. This changes in management roles where the focus is shifted to large-scale project control and client sales.

Retail

The UK retail sector is large, although it is under pressure to change as consumers become more willing to use online marketplaces with home delivery services. This means that roles in online services, marketing and strategy are highly sought after by job seekers but also widely available. These roles often require the co-ordination of logistics functions and groups of personnel to achieve an aim. Many of my colleagues who worked as operations officers have since found careers in major retailers such as Amazon and Ocado where their abilities to allocate scarce resources give them an advantage. These roles can be intensely competitive but the rewards for a job well done have the potential to be significant.

Retailers rely on an efficient supply chain and well- run sales sites, be they physical (shops/stores) or online. When operating correctly these systems are designed to keep costs as low as possible while ensuring a seamless delivery of products to the customer. In addition this same system must facilitate returns from customers and build resilience in case of supplier failure. This industry has clear definitions of operations, sales and logistical roles and regardless of where you work in these divisions (sometimes referred to using the American term "verticals") you are likely to have performance targets to meet.

Retail firms have many varied roles and are comparable to major banks in their willingness to employ former military personnel. They are less concerned about your previous rank and more interested in your credentials as a manager of a system. The larger firms now run military internship schemes which you can apply for even if you left the military some time ago. In my experience they offer some of the most directly transferrable skills from an operations, logistics or human resources focussed military career. There is also likely to be future demand for such skills combined with an strong grounding in computing and technology. The UK online retail sector is predicted to account for half of all UK retail sales by 2028.[30]

Professional services

In simplistic terms this industry comprises those businesses who offer advice and support to other firms for a fee. I include here major and minor consultancies, audit firms (these are companies that will examine the accounts of another business to ensure their accuracy) and single individuals offering bespoke consultancy services.

You may hear of the term "Big 4" which at the time of writing include KPMG, Deloitte, PWC and EY. These are well known accountancy audit firms that have included management consultancy as part of their service portfolio. Accountancy audits occur under a requirement to assure shareholders that the managers of their business are being honest or when a legal requirement for audit exists. In the UK, this legal requirement is enforced when a business qualifies under the Companies Act. The reason for both audit and management consultancy being found in the same business is straightforward. When professional services companies started auditing the financial accounts of their customers they would often notice areas of financial pressure, failure or inefficiency. This would lead to a desire to scrutinise that part of their accounts and naturally led to a desire for management consultancy to change that part of the business or present solutions to the problem.

As a result many audit and accountancy firms began offering management consultancy services. Management consultancy involves many aspects but can be summarised as a service which assesses a particular problem on behalf of a client business then seeks to put forward solutions to that problem, based on research and prior experience. Professional services firms have recognised the value of military experience in this process and offer comprehensive internship programmes and numerous military insight days annually. These are a good way to gain a basic understanding of the firms and to understand what they expect of you.

Management consultancy tends to follow a tried and tested model. The consultancy firm assign teams to projects with mixed personalities and skill sets, led by a senior manager who answers to an account director or partner in the consultancy. A partner is a senior consultant or director who has promoted within the business (or another similar one) and who has progressed to a point where they hold profit sharing rights in the consultancy. As such they have to generate a certain amount of profit each year in order for the business to grow, their position to remain viable and ultimately for their profit sharing total to increase.

In the long-term partnership could become a viable career aim should you remain in the industry. Consultancy firms offer opportunities to travel and an exposure to a wide variety of industries. While many are headquartered in London, there are options to work from offices in other major cities including Bristol, Birmingham, Edinburgh and Liverpool. You can expect be recruited as an "analyst" or "associate" consultant depending on your experience and knowledge of specific sectors/industries. If you have specific experiences in a highly specialised area more senior entry positions may be made available.

American companies with UK bases also offer opportunities. The most notable of these include McKinsey, Bain and Boston Consulting Group (BCG). These are often called "strategic consultancies". Their focus is on large business or government issues and they pride themselves on a reputation for tackling complex national and international problems. With such a reputation and output comes a requirement to work extremely hard under testing circumstances. American firms are highly systematic, making use data and analysis in a manner that leads the global industry in terms of rigour and attention to detail. For a deeper understanding of the requirements and selection process make use of "case interviews" available free online. They require no prior consulting knowledge but are designed to test judgement, basic maths and analysis skills in a management consultancy context. These tests are good mental agility training and will help you to better understand what these businesses do in an applied scenario.

Financial services

The financial services industry has some geographic and cultural parallels with the professional services sector. The main locations globally are in major cities such as London, New York, Paris, Berlin, Hong Kong and Singapore. The industry is split into different types of financial institution, designed to receive money from depositors (you and I in retail banks) and lend money to customers (you and I in the form of mortgages or unsecured loans or businesses through large commercial loans). Additionally investment banking focusses on stock market transactions and business mergers and acquisitions (known in the industry as M&A).

In terms of workload and earning potential, investment banking offers the quickest route to what many would consider the most lucrative positions in the industry. Consequently, this part of the industry has demanding selection processes and the working practices can be akin to being on high-end military operations. The only UK bank with an investment banking division is Barclays, with the remainder being part of American firms such as Goldman Sachs and JP Morgan. All offer military internship programmes and have successfully recruited many former Armed Forces personnel from a range or seniorities and professional backgrounds. For an insight into the workings of an investment bank, Ben Bernanke's autobiography, "The Courage to Act", offers a basic but thorough explanation of how such financial institutions operate.[31] Bernanke was the chairman of the US Federal Reserve (the American equivalent of the Bank of England) during the 2008 financial crisis. His descriptions of key economic indicators are written in plain English as is his description of the Lehman Brothers collapse, the American investment bank whose failure many consider to be the seminal moment of the crisis.

Compliance and operations divisions of the banks are often popular destinations for former military personnel and allow managers to see how new employees in this new environment. These divisions focus on the day to day activities of the bank and police areas such as fraud and money laundering. They also manage the mechanisms by which the bank runs national and global transactions, ensuring that the right money goes to the right account at the right time.

I have often heard these roles described as the equivalent of being a junior officer. If you are not or were not commissioned, do not be put off. I know of successful former leading hands, corporals and lance corporals in both Barclays and JP Morgan and I'm sure there are many. When I considered a career in finance, many advised me to simply take any role I could at the right level and then look to transfer into those I was more interested in once I had established myself. This may sound familiar to many of you from your early stages of applying to the military! There are many variables to consider with such a strategy and relying on internal transfer may not be possible in all cases. Apply for a first role that genuinely appeals and focussing your efforts on succeeding.

The Civil Service

In my latter years of service I spent time working with civil servants, mainly in Westminster. This was an organisation which was new to me and one where I learnt a great deal about wider government structures and the people who serve in them. Like the military, the civil service operates in a public sector hierarchy, with a well defined pension scheme and a widely published pay structure. The opportunities in the civil service are vast and span international boundaries. Almost any qualification or specialism is catered for and once recruited, you can apply for roles which are assessed and awarded through a competency-based interview and application system. This means that those who wish to promote will often move across a wide range of roles and will have opportunities to be exposed to the heart of government.

Many of the organisational advantages and disadvantages which exist in the military are replicated in the civil service, although individuals have more freedom to stay in role or transfer elsewhere when compared to their military counterparts. If the organisational structure or predictable salaries of the military frustrate you, then be prepared for a similar experience, albeit with other advantages. I gained an enormous respect for civil servants in my time working in Westminster. They work under intense pressure and often have a genuine desire to improve things for their country or society. In this sense they many of them have similar motivations to those who serve in the Armed Forces.

Medical Services

Medicine may seem like a strange area to discuss in a book aimed at those transferring from mostly non-medical military careers. Nonetheless, in the spirit of continuous education and personal growth, you may consider re-training as a medical practitioner. Remember, medicine doesn't imply re-training as a doctor. Physiotherapy, nursing, psychology and a host of other areas may be considered under a broader health and well-being career. The military is generally good at teaching those who join how to eat healthily, how to exercise properly and generally facilitate their peak physical performance. This is a good foundation for any follow-on career in medical services, or even attending medical school and re-training completely as a specialist.

Re-training in a medical field will take significant amounts of time and personal investment but the rewards are significant. Seeing positive change in those you help while earning a stable income is appealing to many. The prevalence of medical services across the UK means that you are likely to have access to a role regardless of where you wish to live. As such I advise you to give this area due consideration if you want to contribute to society while learning a new skill, or developing your existing capabilities.

Defence and Security

The defence industry is considered to include major defence companies offering equipment, training and services to governments and occasionally large businesses. Security includes a broad range of services, from on-site surveillance systems and complex cyber activity to physically guarding major installations. There is significant overlap and many large companies operate across both areas. These businesses often contain many of the functions of those in other industries, such as legal, marketing, sales and operations departments. They may also have significant manufacturing capability meaning they straddle the secondary and tertiary sectors.

The largest companies in this sector are referred to as "Primes". This is a common term, short-hand for "Prime-Contractors" and is used in numerous industries. Examples include BAE Systems, QinetiQ, Thales and Boeing Defence UK. These firms are large and may be subsidiaries a foreign parent company (Thales is part owned by the French government; Boeing Defence UK is owned by Boeing in the United States). Many ex-military employees work in these firms, particularly if they have specific knowledge or experience using the equipment that the companies sell to the UK MOD and allied nations.

Working for a large defence or security company may provide you with a more manageable transition from your current role or situation. The language will be familiar and you may even already know people in the business or industry. It is also likely that these firms have offices and bases somewhere near a major transport link or a base where you have served. As such these companies offer you the chance to establish yourself commercially and learn in a comfortable environment rather than working in a new area you know little about. Should you have direct knowledge of the equipment in question you may find yourself in a role known as "business development", where companies expect you to use your network of contacts and knowledge of the company products to generate sales opportunities. This can include meeting with customers, gathering information about industry trends and reacting to them and identifying leads for other parts of the business to pursue. The business development role is common to all industries but service leavers often find themselves in these roles in defence and security firms.

Smaller firms offer opportunity too, particularly if you have specialist experience that they can benefit from. Many smaller defence companies rely on the larger companies to sub-contract to them for specific projects. This means that you could find yourself in a leading project management position or assisting senior parts of a business quickly. These situations provide excellent personal development opportunities as well as giving you access to the higher-level thinking and strategy of the company. It is also likely that you will progress more quickly in a smaller firm like this. As ever this is offset by the risk that you may be paid less and have fewer benefits than your equivalents in larger businesses.

Defence companies are often partnered with military and civil service delivery teams in the procurement process to aid in the delivery of major projects. These opportunities are often arranged through established companies such as BAE Systems or Qinetiq and feed into MOD departments such as Defence Equipment and Support (DE&S) in Bristol. The opportunities here are varied but you could find yourself either in a salaried position or entering these organisations as a contractor on a daily rate of pay. While these rates can be lucrative, remember that as a contractor your job security is limited and that you will be expected to deliver significant outputs to justify your fee. Also note that these rates may be reduced by the agency or firm that places you. By the same token such roles require significant investment in your personal credentials. Project management or engineering qualifications are a common pre-requisite and if this area is of interest, consider achieving these during your remaining time in service. If you have already left and lack these qualifications, consider roles which will allow you to gain them as part of your continuous professional development plan.

In summary, a career in a defence or security business may offer you opportunities for faster progression in a stable setting. You will have opportunities to learn about commercial process while still operating in a semi-familiar environment. This safety and security should be considered in the context of your desires for personal growth and new learning. Examine your options carefully and use your network to full advantage if pursuing a career here.

Legal Services

I include a piece on the legal profession because it is more accessible than many realise and could be immensely rewarding for the right applicant. While many of you will have had no legal training and may never have considered it, there are courses that can set you on this path and a wealth of support from professional bodies and societies.

Those wishing to practice law who have not been qualified in the field before are expected to undertake a Graduate Diploma in Law, or GDL (sometimes called the "Law Conversion"). This course can be studied part-time over 18 months and equips those who pass the final exams with the right foundation to go on to apply for a training contract with an established legal firm. Areas of law are extensive and varied. Should you devote time and maintain focus you could go on to specialise in human rights, maritime trade, family or criminal law. This range also offers some flexibility in where you chose to live. The exception to this would be those who aspire to be barristers rather than solicitors. Barristers have what are known as "higher rights of audience" which means that they can represent defendants or claimants in higher courts and speak on their behalf in front of judges. Barristers are self-employed and work in offices known as "chambers". The largest of these are in London but others exist in regional cities such as Chester and Birmingham.

Training to be either a solicitor or barrister is time consuming and can be expensive. Despite these factors, successful qualification presents opportunities that may be very different from those you are familiar with. Law qualifications are also highly transferrable and those who have some legal experience are often sought after in the business world for contract writing and auditing, deal negotiation and due diligence activity. Every part of our lives is influenced by the law and becoming an expert in it will make you both employable and knowledgeable.

Media

If you have a creative desire that was not satisfied by military service or wish to apply your management or technical skills to a new area, why not consider a media-based career. Whether journalism, television or online content creation there are vast and growing opportunities. In speaking to colleagues and friends this is an area very few military leavers traditionally consider.

There are now dedicated schemes designed to provide an insight into the options available. A friend of mine attended such a course through his career transition package and still works successfully in the industry. There are also approaches that may seem abstract but where your military skills may directly apply. Special effects, aerial filming using un-manned systems and extra or acting roles often require ex-military expertise.

Similarly, writing for a Defence and Security journal, website or even national paper is possible with diligence and hard work. Your network can help here and submitting pieces direct to these publishers and content creators is a good way to advertise your creative capabilities. A feature of this industry is volatility and you could find yourself with unpredictable earnings and periods of intense work followed by gaps in your activity. It is here that the motivation to keep looking for opportunity and grow your industry network will be vital for long-term success.

Which industry is right for you?

An entire book could be written on each industry and I do not intend for this chapter to answer all of your questions in a specific area. The industries listed here are the ones I considered when creating my transition plan. They are a reflection of my military service but also some of the ambitions I held prior to joining the Royal Navy. Re-engaging with these ambitions was a helpful process and had some unexpected positive outcomes.

As a teenager I considered a career as both a lawyer and a civil servant. Despite this, I joined the Royal Navy and trained as a pilot. You may have noticed that the airlines or civilian helicopter work does not feature on my list of potential industries and this is because I did not consider it outside the military. I did, however, explore numerous options that I hadn't considered since I was 19, some of which involved aviation.

The personal lesson was that not all of my military skills were going to be directly transferred into my new career. It is true that I love flying and the industry that surrounds it and I am still engaged with the aviation industry through my business. When considered in isolation though, the act of flying in a commercial sense did not appeal. You may have similar feelings in different areas. There will be skills that you gained from military service which may have obvious applications in the commercial world and which many assume you will use upon entering the job market. In my case it was flying. In your case it could be engineering, medicine or even team-management. If you have a strong desire to work in a certain way and it is disconnected from your previous career, form a plan and devote your energy to making it work. There may be compelling financial or personal reasons for moving directly into a related skill area but if this is not the case explore other options, or find complementary roles.

The same can be said of your previous aspirations. My desire to be a lawyer led me to explore the legal profession when I left military service. I still have an interest in the law and my business partner has ignited an interest in commercial contracts which I hope to develop further. My decision, though, was not to re-train as a legal professional. Examining your previous ambitions in light of your current situation may allow you to find closure on the "what if" moments you could face when your situation is at its most challenging during your transition.

11 WORKPLACE INTEGRATION

The process of finding work, from editing your CV to successfully arriving in post, can be both stressful and rewarding. If like me you had not worked formally outside the military before previously the period of integration into a new workplace can be underestimated. Firstly, you may only have had to integrate once before and it would have been as part of a formalised and highly structured military process. While you are likely to have changed roles while in uniform the core foundations of your experience will have been formed during your initial recruitment. Here your initial norms and values are likely to have stabilised and your experiences during your military career would then be shaped with these subconscious expectations fixed in place. Although I am an entrepreneur my deeply held beliefs had a significant impact on how I perceived working in a commercial rather than public sector environment.

In order to delve deeper into my own experiences of workplace integration I studied a number of theories, both sociological and psychological. Sociology (the study of group behaviour) and psychology (the study of the individual) both play an important role in understanding why we behave in a certain manner. Academia from both fields believe that one perspective has greater influence than the other, but we will not analyse that argument here. Instead, I will highlight to you a theory which in my opinion illustrates neatly the factors most likely to influence your behaviour in your first civilian workplace.

The theory in question is the work of two American University researchers, Bean and Eaton.[32] Their findings focus on psychological influences affecting newly recruited University students. Their aim was to better understand what Universities could do to maximise the chances of retaining students, from the moment their recruitment process began to successful graduation. To do so, they had to first understand the factors affecting student behaviour and decision making before they arrived at University.

I see significant parallels between this situation and the one I faced on leaving the military and entering the civilian job market. A new student is leaving an understood and comfortable environment (family, home, work) and entering another environment with new rules, new geography, new people and perhaps most importantly new objectives. This is a similar transition to joining the military. The difference though is while the military has highly developed procedures for maximising integration quickly, a University (like many civilian employers) does not always have this luxury. This is a generalisation and most academic institutions and large businesses do have professional and well thought out integration processes. Crucially though, they are not as extreme or structured as those you may have experienced before. Bean and Eaton provide a useful handrail when examining our own likely reactions to a new workplace. Identifying personal areas for improvement is a healthy and often liberating experience. It allows you to foresee problems before they arise and most importantly, integrate quickly to achieve professional success in a new role.

The researchers identified numerous factors which exist before an individual enters a new work or academic environment. It is these factors which then act as a bridge with the new organisation to either rapidly integrate them or create a feeling of negativity and ultimately rejection. I have simplified these as follows:

- **Past behaviour and personality**
- **Initial self-confidence**
- **Core beliefs**
- **Coping strategies**
- **Motivation**
- **Skill and ability**

Consider yourself in a new work environment in the context of this list. Whereas those studied by Bean and Eaton had these factors shaped by their adolescence and early years in casual workplaces (such as part-time jobs), you are emerging from an institution which shapes and re-builds these foundational elements from the moment you are recruited.

Your past-behaviour will have been influenced enormously by the nature of service experience. Your personality, while at its core the same as it always has been, will have enhancements and disadvantages stemming from time spent in the military. Personality is a subject of extensive study and research. Have you noticed that many of the people you served with share similar personality traits to you? I did when I was flying. Our squadron was a tight-knit and effective group and part of that effectiveness stemmed from a certain level of predictability in our individual behaviours. This in turn can bring negative outcomes. Similar personality types may be more likely to agree with each other even when difficulties arise which means errors can be missed or ignored more easily. In the civilian workplace you will likely find yourself mixing with a much broader range or personality types to those you were exposed to before. Like you, they will experience pressures and unexpected reactions when presented with a new situation. It is here that understanding your personality to the best of your ability will position you to be sympathetic to others when working with them. It will also help others to understand your short-comings and assist or empathise where appropriate.

The same can be said of your core beliefs. The military is well known for establishing and reinforcing values and standards which are viewed positively in the civilian workplace. You may have held strong beliefs prior to being recruited which have been further shaped or developed with your service. Equally, you may not harbour strong beliefs on any particular matter. I have found it to be a common misconception that everyone in the British military holds very strong core beliefs aligned to a specific way of thinking. In my experience this is not the case. While the majority of servicepeople I have met hold their professional credibility in very high regard, this is not the same as holding a particular moral standpoint on wider issues. This is an important point for those who do not identify with a particularly strong set of core beliefs as there may be a temptation to feel somehow inadequate. Such thinking unnecessary. Each of us hold core beliefs of some kind, but if they are not strong or obvious this need not be a cause for concern.

In this context coping strategies refer to those things we do tolerate an undesirable situation or circumstances that we would otherwise avoid. This may include working with particular character types, carrying out mundane tasks or simply lacking confidence in one's abilities generally. Some coping strategies are obvious. Avoidance of individuals by getting to work before them to make avoid direct contact on arrival. Others are more nuanced and link to the other factors. For example, you might imagine doing something completely different when carrying out a certain set of tasks. The military creates resilience by giving you tools to create coping strategies for difficult situations. Personal fitness develops stamina to cope in situations where sleep is at a premium. Close friendships, forged under uniquely challenging conditions, offer informal support networks that in turn feed personal coping mechanisms.

Using coping strategies to deal with discomfort is certainly not unique to military service. It was a common finding for Bean and Eaton and it is a human trait when forced into positions that result in discomfort. The methods used may be modified depending on the length of time discomfort is experienced for. Analyse how you cope with difficult situations. Are the techniques you use healthy and if so, how might you modify them for your new career? For example, drinking to excess to deal with stress or anxiety is widely believed to be an unhealthy coping strategy. Enrolling in a yoga class or a book club might be new to you, but do not rule out activities such as these if they assist with changes or difficulty in other areas.

Motivation is discussed in the earlier chapters and identifying basic motivating factors will help to target the right organisation or employment method for your future. An area worthy of further consideration in this regard is *"The Theory of Locus of Control*.[33] Originating in the 1960s, Locus of Control theory aims to further understanding in the field of personal motivation and the resulting individual actions. Put simply, the theory poses that we have either an internal or external locus of control. If internal, we are motivated by a belief that we control our own destiny and are individually responsible for personal success or failure. As such, a person with an external locus of control puts greater belief in fate and chance in their success or failure. Their motivations may focus on factors which they believe they cannot control, whereas internally motivated individuals believe they can exercise control over relevant variables and influences. There is a sliding scale and individuals can display elements of both internal and external locus of control or exist at an extreme.

Taking your motivations from the earlier chapters ad now considering them in light of your possible locus of control may be a helpful exercise. I found that I am internally focussed and hold a belief (perhaps naively at times) that I can influence every factor which has an impact on my success or failure. In my case, the main lesson was that chance can sometimes play a role and that there is a small amount of luck in every interaction. I still believe that I can steer my own course but I have been made to think about how luck and chance might have played their part in getting me to my current situation and might continue to do so in the future. If locus of control theory interests you, an internet search will present quizzes to score your motivations against internal and external beliefs. This has the potential to help understand your motivations on a deeper level.

Specific skills and abilities are areas where you likely have a deep understanding of personal strengths and weaknesses. Your career to date will have enhanced your skill base and some will have deep capabilities in fields ranging from engineering, aviation, hospitality and logistics. Consider how the associated skills mesh with your desired future career. If referencing specific qualifications in job applications or business plans, your experience will differ to those entering a new field. As a result, those entering familiar industries may experience less friction than those entering new areas and associated coping mechanisms will vary. An awareness of how "familiar" your new role will feel based on your existing skills aids in preparing for the unexpected and mitigating any risk inherent in your plan.

In the study Bean and Eaton highlight three particular areas they deemed to have the strongest impact on the ability of individuals to integrate with a new environment. These were past behaviour, initial self-confidence and core beliefs. Whether you are serving or have been working in a civilian role for some time, consider how these three areas affect your life. Are you confident? If not, what is holding back your confidence and how might you address this? In my case confidence issues were linked to past experiences in specific areas. My core beliefs are fundamentally similar to the ones I have always held, but they have matured and refined over time. These beliefs, in turn, have shaped the type of work I want now and how I went about transition into the civilian labour market. Linking these three elements together and understanding them in the context of your next steps will help you to optimise your chances of a successful transition.

In order to fully integrate into a new environment and to do so quickly, it is helpful to understand how the factors considered in this chapter can help or hinder. We begin to form impressions of a new work environment from the moment we first interact with the recruitment process. These impressions will create positive and negative feeling that in turn will either bolster our desire to stay or encourage us even at an early stage to begin planning an exit strategy.

Our first impressions can be moulded to match a new environment and create a feeling of commitment through *adaptive strategies.* Such strategies allow us to take seemingly negative emotional reactions to the new environment and mentally create the conditions to succeed. Helpfully the military has a proven record of encouraging the creation and implementation of adaptive strategies among servicepeople. It is the reason why recruits can pass out from challenging training courses and go on to volunteer for even more challenging training later in their careers. The ability to adapt is fundamental to military service and it is here that you can make the most of your previous training in almost any future employment scenario.

On arrival in your new environment your self-confidence levels could be lower than normal. You may also be employing coping strategies to manage increased stress levels and your locus of control will have an impact on where your motivations to stay in this situation (and influence your environment) lie. In order to integrate fully into new employment you will require a combination of increased confidence, reduced stress and an acknowledgement of where your personal locus of control is positioned. There are proven benefits to proactively approaching these elements. Bean and Eaton noted that those who chose to adapt their behaviour to their new University environment most quickly were more likely to stay in higher education and achieve higher marks overall in their studies.

Your integration starts with these foundational elements but continues as social and professional alignment takes place. Unlike the college students in the study, you will have experienced many of these processes in the military. This offers you advantages as you can tailor your lifestyle to match your new working situation while still maintaining the capacity to manage your personal relationships and other commitments. The same was true for me as an entrepreneur with only one "formal" colleague at first (my business partner). This new situation required adaption that I had not expected and which was both liberating and frightening in equal measure.

My first reactions to entrepreneurship were very positive. I felt an unquantifiable sense of freedom and choice that had not been present in the latter stages of my previous career. This was matched by a strong desire to generate business but an associated fear of failure. What if our products and services weren't as desirable as we thought they were? What if the money I had invested was not in fact going to generate a sustainable business? My past behaviours were centred on self-sufficiency and a desire to work outside an institution. Based on this basic analysis I felt that my personality type would be suited to starting and running a business. While I still firmly believe this to be true, there is deeper context which I wish to highlight. Being self-motivated and driven while still employed by the military was straightforward because my salary offered the ultimate safety net should my ideas come to nothing. Making these same decisions after leaving was a very different, but invaluable, experience.

My coping mechanisms centred on keeping as fit as I could and testing new ideas. Having a business partner helped me enormously. I cannot think of a moment where I wavered in my motivation but there were certainly times where I questioned the logic of what I was trying to do. I found that a very closely guarded routine, with regular sleep patterns and a strict diet assisted greatly. Ironically, I became fitter on leaving the military but this was linked to the realisation that I had to look after myself carefully because the free gym and other benefits were gone. During moments of doubt I would re-assess my personal strategy and try to identify areas to improve. I am happy to admit that when I transitioned and began to feel the real stress of commercial pressure for the first time I used coping strategies extensively.

My locus of control has been internally focussed since I was a teenager. This brings significant disadvantages if not properly managed. While I believe very strongly that decisions are the responsibility of individuals and that they control their own path, this has meant I could lack empathy in the past for those who made decision with no alternative courses of action available. I have sometimes made decisions that I didn't want to take but were presented with no control or option to back away. There is also a truism that luck, which is inherently an external factor, plays a part in all of our plans. I have often felt that the military adage *"no plan survives first contact with the enemy"* is another way of saying *"sometimes someone else will get lucky at your expense"*. As such, allowing elements of one's locus of control to be externalised can offer advantages.

The process of integrating into a new environment can appear daunting but keep in mind the countless others who have gone before you and found success at different stages of their second career. If in doubt, ask friends, family or colleagues for advice on your new situation. They will have experienced similar pressures that will help you to understand the difficulties you perceive. Many military re-employment programmes now account for these factors but it will still be prudent to keep in mind the areas where you feel exposed and to address those issues with an open mind.

12 SPECIFIC SKILLS AND AREAS TO CONSIDER

I will now outline some of the skills I focussed on during my final year of service and the associated resources I made use of. This is a guide and it is not definitive but will give you some pointers if you are unsure of how to get started. Use it as a pattern if you wish or create your own plan using my experiences as an example. Learning and personal development is continuous no matter what your personal circumstances.

Basic business principles

I registered for an online course run by London School of Economics and Political Science (LSE). The course I chose claimed to cover the core principles of high-quality Masters in Business Administration but at a fraction of the cost and in only a few weeks. It came at a modest personal expense and I considered it a worthwhile investment in my future. The course proved an excellent starting point and had utility across a number of business areas. Online learning such as this offers a gentle introduction for those who have not been taught about formal business principles and core activities, such as management and financial accounting, vertical integration and budgeting alongside many others. Each short module left me with a host of references (both websites and books) to further my knowledge later on. Many other similar courses are available and I recommend selecting one from a respected institution even if doing so adds a little to the price of the course.

Website design

There are several approaches to creating and managing online services, whether linked to a new business or merely to improve your competence in these areas prior to a new role. For those who aspire to become deep specialists, learning to code is essential. On the other hand, a professional and functional website can be created using a web design platform that requires no coding knowledge. Help is readily available online. I initially subscribed to a well-known domain name and web design service provider which allowed me to buy a website address (domain name) and then access their sponsored website builder. After a couple of days experimenting I became proficient and began creating sites at very low cost.

Much of my learning was fraught with frustration and there were a few nights with very little sleep as I tried to understand my mistakes when my finished sites still didn't look as I had intended. Perseverance was the key and the end result was worth the effort. If all you need is a home page, some information about your business and a "contact me" page, I would recommend this self-teaching method prior to embarking on a more comprehensive online presence.

Marketing

My interpretation of marketing is a personal one. It is merely a tool I use to achieve my business aim and as such I will spend as much or as little time on it as I need to on the journey to achieving and maintaining that aim. That might be an individual sale, continuous revenue or the acquisition of sales rights to an exciting new product.

Some of the technology areas I am interested in are difficult to condense and explain. They are even harder to simplify to a potential customer with whom you may only have thirty seconds to cement your first impression. I follow the mantra that if one cannot explain something simply it is not well enough understood and as such my marketing strategy is focussed on selling the solution to a problem rather than a particular product.

I started by creating one-page briefings on the products and services I aimed to sell (my time as a consultant, a new technology) and quickly realised that a more efficient strategy was required. I then progressed to creating more immersive digital material. This proved both more efficient and effective. There are many approaches to this broad subject and the use of social media seems to be an avenue for some, although it is not my preference. I made use of "Explainer Videos" which are short graphic multimedia pieces created to explain a product or service as quickly and effectively as possible. Their strengths are numerous. They can be posted online many times and to many audiences, have them on a tablet or phone for immediate display to a customer, or incorporate them into presentations. In a similar way to web design, they are straightforward to produce with some hard work and experimentation. Most importantly, they convey information in a consistent and refined manner.

If you aim to start a business, research the marketing strategies of other companies operating in a similar industry or selling a similar product. What advantages do their methods offer to you and how might you emulate those? Are there areas where you would do things differently? Whatever your idea or ambition there will be comparators, both direct and indirect, that you can consider for inspiration or refinement of your existing marketing plans. I also recommend dedicated reading on the subject should you wish to explore this significant area of business further.

Sales

Selling is a refined art rather than a blunt instrument. Sales techniques apply to a wide range of situations, from selling your skills and potential in a job interview to convincing a prospective buyer to spend money on a product you have created yourself. It is an act of influence whereby the salesperson convinces a customer to enter an exchange of resources. This might require hard work, particularly if the customer faces many choices for similar products and services or if the subject of the sale is complex.

We are exposed to sales activity daily as customers. For most, a car or house has been the most significant exposure to a sales team or person. In my experience, both as a customer and entrepreneur, successful selling concentrates on inviting the potential buyer to conclude for themselves that your product or service can solve their problem. This could be through the use of a combination of soft influence tactics and rational ones whereby statistical evidence is introduced to show how your offering can bring benefit in some way. During my early attempts at selling I would include bold statements suggesting that the product would be fundamental to the future success of the customer. I do not know if this came from years of delivering what I hoped were incisive and engaging flight briefs but with some advice and guidance I soon stopped using this technique.

The risk with such an approach is that as a seller, you are suggesting to a potential buyer that what they have been doing or using to date is inadequate. Furthermore, there is an implication that only you have the intelligence or capability to solve their problem. The drawbacks of such an approach are obvious, particularly for a discerning buyer who may feel patronised. Such emotions will subsequently add friction to their decision making which will in turn reduce the likelihood of a sale.

A preferable method is to drop subtle hints that will resonate with an informed or willing customer. This is a product specific activity where the focus remains on leading the customer to conclude that you can help to solve their problem. Certain offerings can be presented simplistically and a good product which fulfils a basic need may sell itself regardless of your approach. For complex technical products products there may an abstract process or feature which needs to be explored carefully and sympathetically if the true value of your offer is to be realised.

As with negotiation and interviewing your personal narrative is very important when selling yourself as a commodity to a potential employer. Your offering to an organisation, whether in the form of your CV or your time can be sold as the solution to a problem or an enhancement to the status quo. Try to take your potential buyer through a story with a logical path and a clear conclusion. The use of abstract concepts can work well if your narrative explains them simply and links them to the end goal. For example, if you have served in many countries for short periods of time with partner nations you can translate your ability to communicate across cultural boundaries into the world of commerce. If you have spent time on submarines, think about how much knowledge you are expected to retain about the functioning of the vessel and how this translates into an ability to retain knowledge across disparate business areas in a complex organisation. The examples are numerous but are only valid if you can validate them with genuine experience.

Basic book-keeping and accountancy software

This subject is particularly pertinent if you plan to start your own business. Put simply, keeping accounts is a legal requirement for any commercial entity in the UK. It allows the government to calculate how much tax you owe based on revenue generated after certain allowable deductions and protects both the government and the business from illegal accounting practices.

The act of keeping a track of sales and costs is often referred to as "book-keeping". Many businesses employ people to do this prior to submitting their consolidated financial statements to qualified accountants when demanded by law. If managing a small business, you may elect to do this yourself. Thankfully there are some intuitive pieces of software which can help you.

While accountancy software often comes with a monthly subscription fee, use of these tools will be likely to reduce your accountancy fees in the long-run and help you track your costs effectively. I will not endorse any software in particular but an internet search will offer numerous options. The software works by producing a formal report based on your sales and expenses which can then be submitted to an accountant alongside receipts and invoices. Book-keeping in this way not only satisfies the requirements of the law but provides a neat manner in which to record your financial activity and minimise time that your accountant has to spend looking for missing receipts and transactions. This (theoretically) results in lower accountancy fees and an efficient financial support system for your business.

Budgeting

Managing a budget is particularly important in a business context. Understanding what is available for spending and how the business plans to use this resource efficiently is vital for survival in both the short and long-term.

Setting a budget based on your savings, borrowing or income will help you to make fully informed decisions. For example, the decision to spend £10,000 with a near guarantee that you can make £100,000 from that investment is a wiser choice than spending £15,000 to make £30,000. Both are valid economic choices but with limited resources, you might not be able to make both. Strictly adhering to a budget allows you to be disciplined in your decision making in business, whether with your own commercial entity or someone else's. If you aim to become a manager later in your career or enter a firm in a senior position you will be presented with budgetary responsibility early on. An understanding of the basic principles now will help you in either situation.

Workplace communication

We have already considered the importance of using specific communications techniques in context. I re-iterate this point because by now you may have a clearer idea of the types of professions or business opportunities that you wish to pursue. With this in mind think again about your communication style and how it applies to your ambition. Do you need to change anything? Perhaps a subtle refinement, or a mixture of communications techniques, will better suit your aims.

If you plan to enter self-employment immediately then you will have to harness a broad spectrum of techniques on a regular basis. For example, my decision to take longer drafting my e-mails has helped me to understand where I was going wrong or habits I had in the military which I do not wish to replicate commercially. Remember, there is only ever one first impression, so do your best to tailor your communication style to your audience. A "one size fits all approach" is unlikely to be effective.

Personal IT support

My use of hardware and software changed as my transition matured. In the military I had a mobile phone and laptop in addition to my own personal IT (which I tended to keep minimal). My view has always been the more systems you try to carry around the more you have to misplace in public.

On the initial setup of my business I had limited my IT to a mobile phone, a laptop and a hard-drive which I backed up based on a set routine. This allowed me to keep track of the large amounts of data I was suddenly trying to manage, from draft CVs, e-mails to and from members of my network and new ideas. I also changed the type of laptop I used. Traditionally I have favoured a larger personal computer, but with the amount of travelling taking place I opted for a smaller, lighter machine that still had a big enough keyboard for me to type comfortably. If you dedicate a laptop to your transition you do not need to spend a lot. I sourced a basic but reliable machine and used it for a limited number of tasks centred on word processing and sending e-mails. I have seen others do the same with a tablet and portable keyboard.

Social media audit

Serving in the military may have already given you a healthy suspicion for what can go wrong if social media is mis-used. It can be extremely damaging and like an e-mail, once material is published it is outside of your control. So too therefore are the consequences of it falling into the hands of a competitor or a potential employer. Sophisticated recruitment agencies and businesses now seek out the online profiles of their applicants to understand how they match either the claims of the CV or the corporate culture of the business in question.

For this reason, I recommend looking very closely at your on-line profiles across all social media platforms. If what you find does not support the professional image or personal credibility you hope to portray, remove it. The same can be said of your use of professional networking platforms such as LinkedIn. These are very useful tools but can do major damage to your reputation and public image if you misuse them. Common errors from spelling mistakes on profiles through to embarrassing images all contribute to the impressions others make before meeting you.

Pacing yourself

In this and the preceding chapters we have covered many subjects, which will offer enough information or result in more research on your part. In conducting this and all related activity, remember the points made earlier in the book regarding energy levels and a manageable routine. If you feel low, depressed or lethargic it is probably linked to over-exertion and cumulative fatigue. At these moments pause for breath. If that means re-setting your routine or taking some time away from your professional preparations, then do so.

Family and friends will be the most likely to notice your fatigue before you do. I have always balanced such advice against my own belief in hard work and perseverance no matter what the cost. While I stand-by these principles I have had to take time to understand how my energy levels are reduced over time and how to re-charge as efficiently as possible. The topics I listed earlier – lack of sleep, social alcohol consumption and a careless diet- are common issues that must be addressed to maximise personal effectiveness. energised and motivated. I encourage you to explore and embrace positive changes to your lifestyle as part of military to civilian transition.

YOUR FUTURE

Having read this book I hope you have some new ideas about the next chapter of your life. Perhaps you will amend a plan you had already, gain confidence knowing that what you thought possible really is, or elect to research a new industry or profession you had not considered. Perhaps you will embark on an adventure you did not think possible and if this is the case I wish you the best of luck.

Change is difficult, which is why some companies sell services helping other companies to implement it. We like to follow familiar patterns and to do things at a certain pace due to our most basic natural instincts. The process you are embarking on will challenge this, resulting in times of great discomfort, regret and even sorrow. Do not fear these moments. Embrace them as part of your development and when the dark times pass, reflect and try to understand what you will do differently in the future. Your offer to the world and to yourself will only strengthen as a result. During transition you will learn much about business interaction and be well placed to pass this knowledge onto those in your position in the future. There is no requirement for you to help other service leavers, but I strongly urge that you do.

I refer now to Samuel Johnson's quote mentioned near the very beginning of this book: "every man thinks meanly of himself for not having been a soldier, or not having been at sea". There is something in this statement that resonates even now for men and women. It is your duty to yourself to take these words, reflect on your past with pride and reach into your future with vigour.

Keep moving forward. Do not stop.

REFERENCES

[1] Bolles R, 2020, *What Colour is Your Parachute,* CA. USA, Ten Speed Press

[2] Boswell J, 1791, *Life of Samuel Johnson*

[3] Minsky H, 1985, *John Maynard Keynes,* McGraw Hill

[4] Fisher and Ury, 2012, *Getting to Yes, negotiating an agreement without giving in*, Great Britain, Random House Publishing

[5] Wilson, 1980

[6] Eleanor Roosevelt, see Blanch Wiesen Cook, Eleanor Roosevelt: The Early Years, 1884-1933 (London: Penguin, 1993)

[7] Brookfield, S, Adult Education: An Overview, in A. Tuinjman eds, *International Encyclopedia of Education*, (Oxford: Pergamon press, 1995)

[8] European Community EPAC https://ec.europa.eu/epale/en/blog/reasons-adult-education

[9] See for example: Ellen A. Skinner & Michael J. Belmont, 'Motivation in the classroom: Reciprocal Effects of Teacher Behaviour and Student Engagement Across the School Year', *Journal of Educational Psychology*, 1993, vol 85, no. 4, pp. 571-581; see also the essays contained within Karthyn R. Wentzel and David B. Miele eds, *Handbook of Motivation at School*, (New York: Routledge, 2009), especially Kathryn R, Wentzel, 'Students' Relationships with Teachers as Motivational Contexts', pp. 301-321; Furrer et al, 'The Influence of Teacher and Peer Relationships on Students' Classroom Engagement and Everyday Motivational Resilience', *National Society for the Study of Education*, 2014, vol

113, 1, pp. 101-123

[10] See the above footnote

[11] Stephen Brookfield, 'Adult Learning: An Overview', *International Encyclopedia of Education*, (Oxford: Pergamum, 1996) pp. 375-380

[12] See Future Learn and Coursera, fee for a one-off course is usually in the area of $30 at time of writing.

[13] Marion Terry, 'Self Directed Adult Learning', *Educational Research Quarterly*, 2006, vol 29.4 pp. 29- 39; see also Brookfield, Adult Learning: an overview'

[14] See Catherine A. Hansman, ' Context – Based Adult Learning', *New Directions for Adult and Continuing Education*, no 89. 2001, pp.43-51

[15] See the above footnote 15

[16] Discussed by both Wilson and Vygotsky in Hansman, ' Context – Based Adult Learning',

[17] See footnote 16

[18] See Hansman, ' Context – Based Adult Learning'

[19] See Terry 'Self Directed Adult Learning by Undereducated Adults'

[20] See the above footnote 21

[21] Christensen C, 2016, *Competing Against Luck*, USA, Harper Collins Publishers

[22] McCormack M, Reprinted 2016 Edition (Original 1984), *What they don't teach you at Harvard Business School*, Profile Books (Main Edition)

[23] Contributors Various, 2017, *Beyond Harvard, All New Street Smarts from the World of Mark H. McCormack*, Profile Books

[24] https://www.economicshelp.org

[25] Department for International Trade, *UK Trade in Numbers*, September 2019, Macro Analysis and Statistics Team (HM Government)

[26] Vance, J D, 2016, *Hillbilly Elegy. A Memoir of a Family and Culture in Crisis*, Great Britain, William Collins Books

[27] *Oxford Dictionary of English*, 2010, Third Edition, Oxford University Press

[28] https://www.bbc.co.uk/news/business-46822706

[29] Lorenz A, 2002, *Kumar Bhattacharyya, The Unsung Guru*, Random House Business Books, First Edition

[30] The Guardian, *Half of UK retail sales will be online within 10 years*, https://www.theguardian.com/business/2019/jul/09/half-of-uk-retail-sales-will-be-online-within-10-years-report-predicts

[31] Bernanke B, 2015, *The Courage to Act, A Memoir of a Crisis and its Aftermath*, USA, W.W.Norton & Co.

[32] Bean J, Eaton S B, 2001, *The Psychology Underlying Successful Retention Prac-*

tices, Baywood Publishing Co

[33] Rooter J, 1966, *Psychological Monographs: General and Applied*, University of Connecticut, Vol. 80, No. 1

ABOUT THE AUTHOR

Alexandre Lovell-Smith

Alex Lovell-Smith spent 12 years as a Royal Navy helicopter pilot and Ministry of Defence procurement officer. Leaving the Royal Navy at the rank of Lieutenant Commander, he is now an entrepreneur. Having joined direct from sixth form, during his military career he studied remotely with the Open University, London School of Economics and Political Science and Kings' College London.

Should you wish to learn more about the book or get in touch about specific subjects covered, please do so to intheserviceof-@gmail.com

Printed in Great Britain
by Amazon